Appetizers

OVER 175 MOUTHWATERING
FIRST COURSES

APPETIZERS

OVER 175 MOUTHWATERING
FIRST COURSES

TED SMART

Specially produced for Ted Smart,
Guardian House, Borough Road,
Godalming, Surrey GU7 2AE

© Salamander Books Ltd., 1993

ISBN 1 85613 901 8

CREDITS

Contributing authors: June Budgen, Lyn Rutherford and
Louise Steele

Introduction by: Sue Felstead

Typeset by: BMD Graphics Ltd, Hemel Hempstead

Colour separation by: Fotographics Ltd, London-Hong Kong,
J. Film Process Ltd. Bangkok, Thailand and
Scantrans Pte. Ltd, Singapore

Photographers: Per Ericson, Paul Grater and Patrick McLeavey

Printed in Italy

Contents

Introduction

Here is a fabulous collection of recipes for the start of a meal or, alternatively, for traditional Italian *Antipasti*, which is a selection of different dishes combined to make a complete meal in itself. The ideas will also appeal to anyone planning a party buffet menu for a special occasion.

To calculate the amount of food needed for a buffet for twelve, use the following menu as a guideline: one meat dish, such as Italian Meat Platter (page 45), one fish or vegetarian savoury dish, such as Baked Stuffed Celery (page 19), a potato, rice or pasta salad, such as Rice Stuffed Tomatoes (page 12), two other salad dishes from the vegetables and salads chapter, a selection of your favourite dessert recipes, including a large bowl of strawberries or raspberries, and finally, a selection of cheeses.

When presenting an hors d'oeuvres platter, make sure the plate is not crowded with too many different dishes. Often one kind of dish attractively arranged on a plate looks better than a mixture.

Buffets are suitable for a variety of different occasions and are particularly popular for barbecues, picnics, late night suppers, children's birthdays and Christenings. Hors d'oeuvres for a drinks party should be 'finger food' that can be picked up and eaten with one hand. Always ensure that napkins are provided for your guests and include a selection of both hot and cold foods. If you are planning a buffet in winter, always try to include a hot dish with cold accompaniments.

Presentation of a buffet is just as important as the food itself. To avoid a confusion of people around the table, make sure the wine and other drinks, cutlery and crockery is placed away from the food itself.

When planning party food, try to select recipes that can be cooked in advance and frozen. Simply reheat the dish just before serving. Suitable dishes for freezing include small quiches, yeast rolls and filo pastries. Any salad dish should be prepared not more than half an hour before serving to keep its freshness.

Some of the simplest appetizers to prepare are Parma Ham with Figs (page 44) or a selection of dips. Carrots, peppers and courgettes all make tasty scoops for tangy dips, as do cauliflower florets, mushrooms, baby sweetcorn and celery. You could also serve cheese straws or little savoury crackers. There are several recipes in the final selection of this book for dips, such as Mexican Bean Dip (page 90) and Minted Sambal Dip (page 92). Alternatively, why not create your own mixture?

Most appetizers can be prepared beforehand and often taste better if they have been refrigerated before serving. If you are planning a menu, it is best to have either a simple appetizer and a more elaborate main course or vice versa. Make sure that you do not overwhelm your guests with an enormous appetizer, followed by a huge main course. Remember, first impressions are often the most lasting, and a carefully chosen appetizer can play a crucial role in any successful dinner party. Happy cooking!

INGREDIENTS

For the most part the recipes in this book call upon everyday ingredients. There are a few specialist ingredients, however, which are worth hunting for in Italian food stores to give your antipasti traditional, authentic flavours.

STORE CUPBOARD INGREDIENTS

Olive oil – the best quality is cold pressed 'Extra Virgin Olive Oil'. Arguably the best source is said to be Lucca in Tuscany but, rather like wine, olive oil will vary from individual groves and from year to year. For salads use rich, green extra virgin olive oil (as a general rule the greener the colour the richer and fruitier the flavour) but for cooking you can use a less expensive olive oil with a blander flavour which will not dominate the other flavours in a dish, or use a mixture of olive oil and either groundnut or sunflower oil. A good quality olive oil can easily be flavoured to give an added dimension to dressings and sauces. Try adding ingredients such as garlic, fresh herbs, lemon peel, chillies, peppercorns or other spices. A traditional example of this is 'Olio Santo' (Holy Oil) where the best extra virgin olive oil is flavoured with fresh basil and hot red chilli peppers.

Olives – green olives are unripe, black ones fully ripe, you can buy them preserved in brine or in oil. They are widely available in many forms – whole or stoned, or stuffed with ingredients such as pimentos, anchovy fillets or almonds.

Olive paste – made from green or black olives ground to a paste with a little olive oil and seasonings. Olive paste can be bought in jars from supermarkets, delicatessens and Italian food stores, but it is very easy to make yourself. Simply process stoned olives in a blender or food processor, adding seasoning and just enough good quality oil to make a fairly smooth paste. Store in small jars, keep fresh and airtight by covering with a layer of olive oil. (A small jar prepared in this way can be kept, refrigerated, for about 3 months). Olive paste is delicious as a snack or simple antipasto on toast, tossed with pasta, or served as a dip.

Balsamic vinegar – more expensive than wine vinegars, but with a rich, sweet aromatic flavour. The price will vary enormously according to the length of time the vinegar has been matured. The more mature vinegars are more concentrated and so can be used very sparingly. A few drops is often all that is required to flavour a dressing.

Sun-dried tomatoes – when these are specified in a recipe those packed in oil in jars have been used. Their concentrated, salty, tomato flavour is good in salads, on bread with cheeses, and chopped into dressings and dips. Sun-dried tomatoes can also be bought loose in the dry state but they will need to be reconstituted before they are used. Put the pieces of tomato in a bowl, pour over boiling water and leave for 1-1½ hours; they will soften but still be chewy. Drain well and dry on absorbent kitchen paper.

Sun-dried tomato paste – with a richer flavour than ordinary tomato paste, sun-dried tomato paste is a really useful store cupboard ingredient. It transforms sauces and soups and makes a quick pizza topping. Used sparingly with basil and garlic, it becomes a sauce for pasta and makes a superb savoury when thinly spread on hot toasted bread.

Capers in wine vinegar – have a sharp aromatic flavour that is a perfect contrast to oily fish, eggs, fried and rich foods. Look for those preserved in wine vinegar as others can have a harsh, vinegary taste.

Red and yellow peppers (capsicums) in wine vinegar – have a sweet sour flavour. They are a useful store cupboard stand-by as it is easy to use just a small piece as a garnish, cut into strips or dice. The vinegar can be used as a flavouring.

Porcini (dried ceps) – are essential for all mushroom recipes where the strong, earthy flavour of wild mushrooms is desired. Buy porcini in small packets (a little goes a long way) from Italian delicatessens and use in rice dishes, sautées and stuffings. To reconstitute before using, put the porcini in a small bowl, pour over boiling water and leave for 20-30 minutes. Drain, reserving the soaking liquor, then rinse the porcini. Chop them for use. Use the soaking liquor, as a wonderful mushroomy stock.

1 sun-dried tomatoes; 2 sun-dried tomato paste; 3 porcini; 4 red and yellow peppers (capsicums) in wine vinegar; 5 capers; 6 stuffed olives; 7 black olive paste; 8 green olive paste; 9 green and black olives.

CHEESE

Mozzarella – true mozzarella is made from buffalo milk, but today most of what we buy is made from cows' milk. This is fine for cooked dishes, on pizzas and with pasta, but for salads or for eating on its own as a dessert cheese it is worth paying more for full-flavoured, more creamy textured mozzarella di bufala.

Parmesan – the most famous matured hard cheese of Italy, Parmesan is most often used for grating over pasta, risottos, sauces and other cooked dishes, but it is also superb in salads and as a table cheese. Always buy Parmesan in a piece to be cut or grated as needed.

The drums of ready-grated Parmesan cheese that are available simply do not compare in flavour.

Pecorino – is a hard cheese which has a fairly strong distinctive taste. It is used and eaten in the same way as Parmesan. Pecorino is available in several varieties such as Pecorino Sardo, made in Sardinia; Pecorino Romano; Pecorino Toscano; and Pecorino Pepato which is spiced with peppercorns.

Provolone – is made in a variety of shapes such as oval, cone and pear shaped which are hung by cords to ripen. Young mild 'provolone dolce' is most often eaten as a table cheese while the stronger, mature 'provolone piccante' is usually used in cooking.

Fontina – a semi-hard cheese with a natural brown rind, creamy texture and a sweet, nutty flavour. Fontina is considered a fine table cheese but it is also a good cooking cheese and its popular use is in the hot cheese fondue of the Piedmont region 'Fonduta'.

Gorgonzola – a mild blue-veined cheese with a pleasantly sharp flavour made in the town of the same name in the Lombardy region of Italy.

Dolcelatte – is a factory made version of Gorgonzola. It has a creamier flavour as its name suggests – dolcelatte translates to 'sweet milk'.

Mascarpone – a fresh unripened cheese made from curdling thick cream with citric acid, heating and whipping it. It is very rich, and has a thick velvety texture. Mascarpone is available in tubs in large supermarkets and delicatessens. It is often served sweetened and flavoured with liqueurs as a dessert but its luxurious flavour and texture are good in savoury dishes too.

SAUSAGES AND CURED MEATS

Salami – there are countless varieties of Italian salami, each region having its own specialities. Italian salamis are made of raw ingredients which are cured by brine-pickling and/or smoking. The following examples are

1 Italian pork cooking sausages; 2 Prosciutto; 3 Coppa di Parma; 4 Salami (Felino); 5 Salami (Napoli); 6 Bresaola; 7 Mortadella.

1 Ricotta; 2 Mozzarella; 3 Dolcelatte; 4 Fontina; 5 Parmesan; 6 Provolone; 7 Pecorino di Sardo; 8 Mascarpone; 9 Pecorino.

available outside Italy and are well worth looking for in delicatessens and Italian food shops.

Milano – fairly fine in texture, this large salami, is made from minced pork or a mixture of pork and beef.

Varzi – coarse and highly spiced and seasoned, this salami is produced in the village of Varzi in the Parma region.

Felino – a long, thin, pork salami, coarse in texture with a good flavour. Felino is always sliced on the diagonal.

Finocchiona – a large, pure pork salami distinctively flavoured with fennel seeds. It comes from Tuscany.

Prosciutto – salted and air-dried raw ham. Parma Ham is the most famous of these cured meats but other regions produce their own versions.

Bresaola – sold thinly sliced, bresaola is raw beef which has been salted and air-dried in the same way as prosciutto.

Coppa di Parma – like prosciutto di Parma this is salted and air-dried raw ham but it is the shoulder cut rather than the hind leg. The flavour is slightly sweeter than prosciutto.

Mortadella – the largest and probably the most famous Italian sausage. The best mortadella is made from pure pork but others may contain some beef or offal. The spices and flavourings can vary and mortadella may contain whole black peppercorns, coriander seeds, stoned olives or pistachio nuts. It is usually served very thinly sliced, but it may also be diced and added to salads or cooked dishes.

BEAN & ONION SALAD

350 g (12 oz) French beans, topped and tailed
1 onion, thinly sliced
2 tablespoons capers in vinegar, drained
6 tablespoon extra virgin olive oil
Juice 1 lemon
½ teaspoon hot red pepper flakes
Pinch granulated sugar
Salt and freshly ground black pepper
2 teaspoons chopped fresh Italian parsley
1 teaspoon chopped fresh mint

Cook beans in boiling salted water for 3-4 minutes so they remain crisp. Drain and refresh under cold running water. Drain well. Place in a bowl with onion and capers.

Put olive oil, lemon juice and red pepper flakes, sugar, salt and ground black pepper, in a small bowl or screw-top jar. Beat or shake together to mix well.

Add dressing and herbs to salad, mix well.

Serves 4-6.

ASPARAGUS & EGG SALAD

1 kg (2 lb) asparagus
7 eggs, hard-boiled
6 tablespoons olive oil
2 tablespoons white wine vinegar
2 small pickled gherkins, finely chopped
Salt and freshly ground black pepper
Chopped fresh Italian parsley and sprigs to garnish

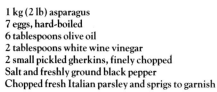

Snap off and discard woody ends of asparagus stems. Using a small, sharp knife, scrape stems, rinse then tie into small bundles using string.

Stand bundles upright in a deep pan of boiling salted water so tips are above water. Cover, making a dome of foil, if necessary. Boil for 15 minutes until tips are just tender. Drain, refresh under cold running water, drain, untie bundles and leave to cool.

Finely chop four hard-boiled eggs and place in a bowl. Using a wooden spoon stir in oil, vinegar and gherkins. Season with salt and ground black pepper. Set aside. Quarter remaining eggs and arrange with asparagus around edge of a serving plate. Pour egg sauce into centre and sprinkle with chopped Italian parsley. Garnish with Italian parsley sprigs.

Serves 4-6.

GRILLED PEPPER SALAD

1 large red pepper (capsicum)
1 large green pepper (capsicum)
1 large yellow pepper (capsicum)
1 small red onion, sliced
16 black olives
2 teaspoons chopped fresh basil
2 teaspoons chopped fresh thyme
DRESSING:
3 tablespoons extra virgin olive oil
1 tablespoon red wine vinegar
1 clove garlic, finely chopped
Pinch granulated sugar
Salt and freshly ground black pepper

To make dressing, mix all ingredients together in a small bowl, or shake together in a screw-top jar. Set aside. Preheat grill. Place whole peppers (capsicum) under hot grill for about 10 minutes, turning occasionally, until skins are evenly blistered and charred. Transfer peppers to a plastic bag for a few minutes, then peel away and discard skins.

Cut peppers in half, discard seeds and cut into strips. Place in salad bowl with onions and olives. Shake dressing and pour over salad. Toss gently to mix and sprinkle over herbs.

Serves 4.

MUSHROOMS & BUTTER BEANS

225 g (8 oz) dried butter beans, soaked overnight and
    drained
225 g (8 oz) button mushrooms, thinly sliced
55 g (2 oz) piece Parmesan cheese
1 tablespoon finely chopped fresh Italian parsley
Lettuce leaves to garnish, if desired
DRESSING:
5 tablespoons extra virgin olive oil
Finely grated peel ½ lemon
½ teaspoon wholegrain mustard
Pinch granulated sugar
Salt and freshly ground black pepper

Put beans in a large saucepan with plenty of water to cover. Bring to the boil and boil briskly for 10 minutes then lower heat, cover and simmer for about 40-45 minutes or until the beans are tender. Drain and rinse under cold running water. Drain well and leave until cold. To make dressing, put all ingredients in a small bowl or put into a screw-top jar and stir or shake together. Set aside.

Put beans and mushrooms in a large serving bowl. Pour over dressing and toss well to mix. Leave for up to 2 hours, if desired. Using a small, sharp knife, pare wafer-thin slices of Parmesan, add to salad and toss lightly to mix. Sprinkle over chopped Italian parsley, garnish with lettuce leaves, if desired, and serve immediately.

Serves 6.

MIXED BEAN SALAD

RICE-STUFFED TOMATOES

115 g (4 oz) dried cannelini beans, soaked overnight
  and drained
115 g (4 oz) dried black eyed beans, soaked overnight
  and drained
115 g (4 oz) dried broad beans, soaked overnight and
  drained
1 small onion, chopped
2 tablespoons chopped fresh oregano
1 tablespoon chopped fresh Italian parsley
DRESSING:
4 tablespoons extra virgin olive oil
2 tablespoons red wine vinegar
2 cloves garlic, crushed
Salt and freshly ground black pepper
Fresh Italian parsley sprigs to garnish

6 large, ripe tomatoes
115 g (4 oz/⅔ cup) risotto rice or long-grain white rice
3 50 ml (12 fl oz/1½ cups) boiling chicken stock
4 tablespoons olive oil
1 small onion, finely chopped
1 clove garlic, crushed
225 g (8 oz) fresh spinach, finely chopped
3 tablespoons chopped fresh Italian parsley
Salt and freshly ground black pepper
Mixed salad leaves to serve

Cut tops off tomatoes and reserve. Using a
teaspoon scoop out tomato seeds and flesh;
reserve flesh for use in sauces or casseroles.
Place tomatoes upside down to drain.

Put beans in separate saucepans. Cover with
cold water, bring to the boil and boil briskly
for 10 minutes then lower the heat and simmer, covered, for about 1 hour until just
tender. Drain, rinse under cold running water
then drain and transfer to a serving dish.

Preheat oven to 180C (350F/Gas 4). Rinse
rice and put in a small saucepan with boiling
chicken stock. Bring to the boil then lower
heat, cover and simmer gently for 12-15
minutes until liquid is absorbed. If rice is not
tender stir in a little boiling water and
continue cooking. Meanwhile, heat 2 tablespoons of the oil in a medium saucepan. Add
onion and garlic and sauté for 3 minutes to
soften.

Meanwhile, to make dressing mix ingredients
together in a small bowl until evenly blended, or shake together in a screw-top jar. Add
onion and dressing to beans while they are
warm. Stir and allow to cool completely.
Chill until required. Just before serving, stir
in oregano and parsley and adjust seasoning.
Garnish with Italian parsley sprigs.

Serves 6.

Stir in spinach, parsley and cooked rice.
Remove from heat and season with salt and
freshly ground black pepper. Sprinkle tomato
insides with salt, then fill with rice mixture.
Replace reserved tomato tops. Arrange in a
baking dish and sprinkle with remaining oil.
Bake in the preheated oven for 20 minutes
until tomatoes are tender. Serve hot or cold
with salad leaves.

Serves 6.

AUBERGINE NAPOLETANA

700 g (1½ lb) medium thin aubergine (eggplant)
Salt
115 g (4 oz/1 cup) plain (all-purpose) flour
225 ml (8 fl oz/1 cup) groundnut oil
225 ml (8 fl oz/1 cup) olive oil
115 ml (4 fl oz/½ cup) extra virgin olive oil
6 anchovy fillets canned in oil, drained and mashed
1 tablespoon sun-dried tomato paste
3 tablespoons red wine vinegar
8 sprigs fresh Italian parsley
2 cloves garlic
Salt and freshly ground black pepper
Fresh Italian parsley sprigs, to garnish

Peel aubergines (eggplant) and cut into 2.5 cm (1 inch) slices. Spread out on a large plate and sprinkle with plenty of salt. Leave to stand for 30 minutes then rinse thoroughly under cold running water. Drain and pat dry with absorbent kitchen paper.

Put flour into a large plastic bag. Add aubergine (eggplant) and toss to coat. Remove coated aubergine (eggplant) and discard excess flour.

Preheat groundnut and olive oil together in a saucepan or deep-fat fryer to 190C (375F). Deep-fry aubergines (eggplant) in batches in the hot oil for about 4 minutes until golden brown. Transfer to absorbent kitchen paper to drain. Keep hot.

In a small saucepan, gently warm extra virgin olive oil over a low heat. Stir in anchovies, sun-dried tomato paste and vinegar and simmer, stirring, for 2 minutes.

Finely chop together parsley and garlic. Transfer aubergines (eggplant) to a warmed serving plate. Pour over anchovy sauce and season with salt and freshly ground black pepper. Sprinkle with chopped parsley and garlic and serve immediately garnished with Italian parsley sprigs.

Serves 4-6.

— BROCCOLI & PROSCIUTTO —

700 g (1½ lb) broccoli
225 g (8 oz) tomatoes
3 tablespoons olive oil
.150 g (5 oz) prosciutto, cut into strips
2 cloves garlic, chopped
55 g (2 oz/⅓ cup) pine nuts, toasted
12 stoned black olives, halved
Salt and freshly ground black pepper
8 sprigs fresh basil

Divide the broccoli into fairly large flowerets. Add to a saucepan of boiling, salted water and cook for about 4 minutes, until just tender. Drain, refresh under cold running water, then drain well.

Meanwhile, put tomatoes in a bowl and pour on boiling water to cover. Leave to stand for about 30 seconds. Drain, cool under cold running water then peel away skins. Cut the tomatoes into chunks and discard seeds. Heat 2 tablespoons of the oil in a frying pan. Add the prosciutto and garlic and fry over a high heat for a few minutes until the prosciutto is crisp. Using a slotted spoon transfer prosciutto to a plate and keep warm.

Add the remaining oil to the pan with the tomatoes, pine nuts and olives. Cook, stirring, for 1 minute. Stir in broccoli and prosciutto and heat through briefly, gently stirring. Season with salt and freshly ground black pepper. Transfer to a warmed serving dish and sprinkle with basil leaves. Serve hot.

Serves 4-6.

— BAKED STUFFED ARTICHOKES —

4 large young artichokes
3 tablespoons fresh white breadcrumbs
25 g (1 oz/¼ cup) pecorino cheese, grated
Juice 1 lemon
5 tablespoons olive oil
15 g (½ oz) butter
2 tablespoons olive oil
3 slices lean bacon, chopped
1 small onion, finely chopped
2 sticks celery, finely chopped
2 medium courgettes (zucchini), finely chopped
1 clove garlic, crushed
1 tablespoon chopped fresh sage
1 tablespoon chopped fresh Italian parsley
Salt and freshly ground black pepper
Fresh Italian parsley sprigs to garnish

Preheat oven to 200C (400F/Gas 6). Cook artichokes in a saucepan of boiling salted water for 30 minutes. Remove and place upside down to drain. Pull away and discard outer leaves and, using a teaspoon, remove central hairy choke. Heat butter and 2 tablespoons olive oil in a saucepan. Add bacon, onion, celery, courgette (zucchini) and garlic and cook gently for 5 minutes, stirring frequently, until vegetables are just soft. Stir in herbs. Pureé half the mixture in a food processor or blender. Return to pan. Season with salt and freshly ground black pepper.

Place artichokes close together in an ovenproof dish. Fill centres of artichokes with vegetable mixture. In a small bowl, mix together breadcrumbs and cheese. Pile on top of filling. Sprinkle with lemon juice and remaining 3 tablespoons olive oil. Cover with foil and bake in the preheated oven for 15 minutes. Remove foil. Bake for a further 10 minutes until lightly browned. Serve garnished with Italian parsley sprigs.

Serves 4.

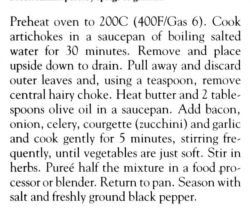

STUFFED ARTICHOKE BOTTOMS

6 hard-boiled eggs, finely chopped
7 - 9 tablespoons extra virgin olive oil
2 tablespoons white wine vinegar
½ red pepper (capsicum) packed in wine vinegar,
    drained and chopped
2 tablespoons capers in wine vinegar, drained and
    chopped
2 tablespoons chopped fresh Italian parsley
Salt and freshly ground black pepper
400 g (14 oz) can artichoke bottoms, drained
3 tablespoons extra virgin olive oil
Juice ½ lemon
1 teaspoon coriander seeds, crushed
Fresh Italian parsley sprigs to garnish

Place eggs in a bowl then, using a wooden spoon, gradually stir in 4 tablespoons of the oil and the vinegar; the mixture should be stiff enough to hold its shape but if too dry add a little more olive oil. Stir in pepper, capers and parsley and season with salt and freshly ground black pepper.

Divide egg mixture between artichoke bottoms and arrange on a serving plate. Trickle over remaining olive oil and lemon juice and sprinkle with coriander seeds. Chill for at least 1 hour. Serve garnished with Italian parsley sprigs.

Serves 4-6.

── CAULIFLOWER INSALATA ──

1 cauliflower
55 g (2 oz) stoned green olives, halved
55 g (2 oz) stoned black olives, halved
2 tablespoons capers in wine vinegar, drained
1 red pepper (capsicum) packed in wine vinegar drained
    and chopped
5 anchovy fillets, canned in oil, drained and halved
    crosswise
6 tablespoons extra virgin olive oil
1 tablespoon white wine vinegar
Salt and freshly ground black pepper
3 small carrots

Break the cauliflower into flowerets.

Cook cauliflower in boiling salted water for 4-5 minutes until crisp. Drain and refresh under cold running water. Drain and leave to cool. Put cauliflower, olives, capers, red pepper (capsicum) and anchovies into a serving bowl. Add oil and vinegar and season with salt and freshly ground black pepper. Toss gently and chill for at least 30 minutes.

Using a potato peeler, remove long thin shreds from carrots. Place shreds in a bowl of iced water for 10 minutes to curl and crisp. Drain well and add to salad. Toss lightly then serve.

Serves 6.

FUNGHETTO

225 g (8 oz) aubergine (eggplant), diced
225 g (8 oz) courgettes (zucchini), thinly sliced
15 g (½ oz) dried ceps (porcini)
25 g (1 oz) butter
4 tablespoons olive oil
2 cloves garlic, crushed
225 g (8 oz) button or oyster mushrooms, or a mixture, sliced
2 tablespoons fresh rosemary leaves
2 tablespoons chopped fresh Italian parsley
Salt and freshly ground black pepper
Fresh rosemary sprigs to garnish

Put aubergine (eggplant) and courgette (zucchini) in a colander.

Sprinkle with plenty of salt and leave to drain for 30 minutes. Rinse thoroughly to remove salt and drain on absorbent kitchen paper. Put dried ceps (porcini) in a small bowl. Cover with warm water and set aside for 20 minutes. Strain, reserving 3 tablespoons soaking liquor. Rinse ceps (porcini) thoroughly and chop.

Heat butter and oil in a large, heavy frying pan. Add garlic and sauté for 1 minute. Add aubergine (eggplant) and courgette (zucchini), mushrooms, ceps (porcini) and rosemary. Sauté for 3-4 minutes. Stir in reserved soaking liquor and the parsley, lower heat and cook for 20-25 minutes until vegetables are soft and liquid evaporated. Season with salt and ground black pepper and garnish with rosemary sprigs.

Serves 4-6.

COURGETTES WITH GARLIC

6 medium-sized courgettes (zucchini)
225 ml (8 fl oz/1 cup) corn or groundnut oil
225 ml (8 fl oz/1 cup) olive oil
2 cloves garlic, chopped
70 ml (2½ fl oz/⅓ cup) red wine vinegar
1-2 tablespoons chopped fresh dill
Salt and freshly ground black pepper
12 fresh mint leaves

Preheat oven to 190C (375F/Gas 5). Using a potato peeler and pressing fairly firmly, peel along the lengths of courgettes (zucchini) to remove long, thick 'ribbons'. Divide between two baking sheets and bake in the preheated oven for 20 minutes until just tender.

Transfer courgettes (zucchini) to absorbent kitchen paper to drain for 30 minutes. Half-fill a saucepan or deep-fat fryer with the oils and heat to 190C (375F). Line a baking sheet with absorbent kitchen paper. Fry courgette (zucchini) slices in batches in the hot oil for 2-3 minutes until a light golden brown. Using a slotted spoon, transfer to prepared baking sheet to drain. When all courgettes (zucchini) are cooked and drained transfer to a serving dish.

Add garlic, red wine vinegar, chopped dill and salt and freshly ground black pepper to courgettes (zucchini). Toss gently to mix. Cover and leave in refrigerator for at least 2 hours. Serve sprinkled with mint leaves.

Serves 6.

MUSHROOMS BAKED IN MARSALA —— ITALIAN FRITTERS

55 g (2 oz) butter
450 g (1 lb) large button mushrooms, thickly sliced
2 cloves garlic, sliced
150 ml (5 fl oz/⅔ cup) marsala
Salt and freshly ground black pepper
Chopped fresh Italian parsley to garnish

Preheat oven to 190C (375F/Gas 5). Use butter to grease a large flat baking dish.

Layer mushrooms in dish and sprinkle over garlic slices.

Pour marsala over mushrooms and season with salt and freshly ground black pepper. Bake in the preheated oven for 25-30 minutes until mushrooms are tender. Serve hot or cold, sprinkled with Italian parsley.

Serves 4.

Note: For a special occasion or a treat substitute fresh ceps (porcini) for some of the button mushrooms.

6 small courgettes (zucchini) with flowers
175 g (6 oz) oyster mushrooms
4 tablespoons balsamic vinegar
4 tablespoons extra virgin olive oil
1 tablespoon chopped fresh basil
Salt and freshly ground black pepper
Sifted flour for coating
Vegetable oil for deep frying
BATTER:
1 egg, lightly beaten
225 ml (8 fl oz/1 cup) ice-cold water
115 g (4 oz/1 cup) plain (all-purpose) flour, sifted
Fresh basil leaves to garnish

Break flowers off courgettes (zucchini).

Slice each courgette (zucchini) lengthwise into three strips. Cut large mushrooms into halves or quarters; leave others whole. Put vinegar in a small bowl for dipping. In a separate small bowl mix together olive oil, basil, salt and freshly ground black pepper. Set both aside. To make batter, in a bowl, stir together egg and water. Gently mix in flour to get the consistency of light cream.

Half-fill a deep-fat frying pan or saucepan with oil; preheat to 180C (350F). Dip courgettes (zucchini) strips and flowers, and mushrooms into sifted flour to coat. Shake off excess. Dip a few pieces of floured vegetables at a time, in batter then deep fry in hot oil for 3-4 minutes, turning frequently, until golden. Drain on absorbent kitchen paper. Season with salt and garnish with basil leaves. Serve with the bowls of balsamic vinegar and flavoured oil.

Serves 4-6.

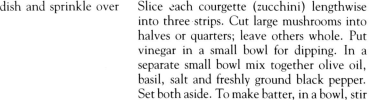

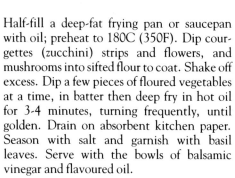

PEPERONATA

2 green peppers (capsicums)
1 red pepper (capsicum)
700 g (1½ lb) tomatoes, peeled, seeded and roughly
  chopped
85 ml (3 fl oz/⅓ cup) olive oil
1 onion, roughly chopped
1 clove garlic, crushed
Pinch granulated sugar
Salt and freshly ground black pepper
1 tablespoon chopped fresh Italian parsley

Preheat grill. Put peppers (capsicums) under the hot grill and cook for about 10 minutes, turning occasionally, until skins are evenly blistered and charred.

Transfer to a plastic bag for a few minutes then peel away and discard skins. Cut peppers (capsicums) in half, discard seeds and cut into strips. Heat oil in a large frying pan. Add onion and garlic and cook gently for 3 minutes to soften.

Stir in tomatoes and sugar and cook gently for 10-12 minutes until thickened. Increase heat if necessary. Add peppers (capsicums) strips and simmer gently for 5 minutes until peppers are soft. Season with salt and freshly ground black pepper and serve hot sprinkled with chopped Italian parsley.

Serves 4.

ARUGULA & PINE NUT SALAD

55 g (2 oz/⅓ cup) pine nuts
85 g (3 oz) arugula (roquette)
4 spring onions (scallions), thinly sliced
8 sprigs fresh chervil, roughly torn
2 thin slices Parma ham, cut into strips
DRESSING:
Juice 1 lemon
3 tablespoons extra virgin olive oil
1 tablespoon walnut oil
½ teaspoon Dijon mustard
Salt and freshly ground black pepper

In a small saucepan heat pine nuts, without oil, over a medium heat, stirring continuously for about 3 minutes until golden brown.

Remove nuts to a plate and set side to cool. Place arugula, spring onions (scallions), chervil and ham in a serving bowl. Toss gently to mix.

To make dressing, mix ingredients together in a small bowl until evenly blended or shake together in a screw-top jar. Pour over salad and toss. Sprinkle over reserved pine nuts.

Serves 4-6.

TOMATO & RED ONION SALAD

4 beefsteak tomatoes, sliced
4 sun-dried tomatoes packed in oil, drained and
    chopped
1 red onion, chopped
Salt and freshly ground black pepper
3 tablespoons extra virgin olive oil
2 tablespoons oil from the sun-dried tomatoes
2 tablespoons red wine vinegar
Pinch granulated sugar
4 tablespoons chopped mixed fresh herbs, such as basil,
    oregano, parsley, chives, dill and coriander
Fresh herb sprigs to garnish

BAKED STUFFED CELERY

1 head celery, separated into sticks and cut into 7.5 cm
    (3 in) lengths
55 ml (2 fl oz/¼ cup) olive oil
STUFFING:
3 tablespoons olive oil
1 small onion, finely chopped
1 clove garlic, chopped
2 tablespoons capers in wine vinegar, drained
1 red pepper (capsicum) packed in wine vinegar,
    drained
25 g (1 oz/½ cup) fresh white breadcumbs
55 g (2 oz/1½ cup) provolone cheese, grated
3 tablespoons chopped fresh Italian parsley
Salt and freshly ground black pepper
Fresh Italian parsley to garnish

Layer tomatoes, sun-dried tomatoes and onion in a shallow serving dish. Season with salt and freshly ground black pepper.

Preheat oven to 190C (375F/Gas 5). Add celery to large saucepan of boiling water and cook for 3 minutes. Drain and refresh under cold running water. Drain and leave to dry on absorbent kitchen paper. To make stuffing, heat oil in a frying pan. Add onion and garlic and cook gently for 3 minutes to soften. Remove from the heat. Chop together capers and red pepper (capsicum) then stir into frying pan with breadcrumbs, cheese and parsley. Season with salt and freshly ground black pepper.

Mix together remaining ingredients, except garnish, in a small bowl then pour over the salad. Serve garnished with fresh herb sprigs.

Serves 4-6.

Place stuffing in cavities of celery pieces. Arrange, stuffing upwards, in one layer in a shallow baking dish. Trickle oil over. Cover with foil and bake in the preheated oven for 20 minutes. Remove foil and continue cooking for about 10 minutes until celery is tender and stuffing lightly browned. Serve hot or warm garnished with Italian parsley.

Serves 6.

TRICOLOR SALAD

1 avocado
1 tablespoon lemon juice
2 large beefsteak tomatoes
175 g (6 oz) mozzarella cheese
Salt and freshly ground black pepper
Few drops balsamic vinegar
4 tablespoons extra virgin olive oil
6 basil leaves, shredded
Fresh basil sprigs to garnish

Stone and peel avocado, slice thinly and brush with lemon juice.

Arrange tomatoes, mozzarella and avocado on a large serving plate. Sprinkle over salt and freshly ground black pepper.

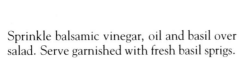

Sprinkle balsamic vinegar, oil and basil over salad. Serve garnished with fresh basil sprigs.

Serves 4-6.

COURGETTE & TOMATO SALAD

About thirty 5 cm (2 in) long courgettes (zucchini), total weight about 450 g (1 lb)
350 g (12 oz) small tomatoes, sliced
4 spring onions (scallions), white part only, sliced
1 tablespoon chopped fresh Italian parsley
DRESSING:
5 tablespoons extra virgin olive oil
3 tablespoons white wine vinegar
2 cloves garlic, chopped
1 tablespoon chopped fresh thyme
1 teaspoon clear honey
Salt and freshly ground black pepper

Add courgettes (zucchini) to a saucepan of boiling salted water and cook for 3 minutes. Drain well. Using a small, sharp knife, cut a long lengthwise slit in each courgette (zucchini) and place in a serving dish.

To make dressing, mix ingredients together in a small bowl, or shake together in a screw-top jar. Pour over hot courgettes (zucchini) and leave until completely cold. Add tomatoes, spring onions (scallions) and parsley to dish. Toss to mix. Adjust seasoning before serving.

Serves 6.

FENNEL & DOLCELATTE

3 medium bulbs fennel
1 tablespoon fennel seeds, lightly crushed
4 tablespoon extra virgin olive oil
Juice ½ lemon
Pinch granulated sugar
Salt and freshly ground black pepper
115 g (4 oz) dolcelatte cheese

Trim fennel, reserving green feathery tops. Add whole bulbs to a saucepan of boiling salted water, cook for 5 minutes, then drain. Refresh under cold water, drain well then pat dry with absorbent kitchen paper; set aside. Chop reserved fennel tops and set aside.

In a small frying pan over medium heat, dry-fry fennel seeds for 2-3 minutes to brown and release aroma. Remove from the heat and stir in olive oil, lemon juice, sugar, salt and ground black pepper.

Thinly slice fennel bulbs and arrange in a shallow serving dish. Pour over oil and fennel seed mixture. Crumble cheese and sprinkle over salad with reserved fennel tops. Leave to stand for 30 minutes. Toss lightly before serving.

Serves 4-6.

EGG & ARTICHOKE SALAD

4 eggs, hard-boiled, quartered
12 artichoke hearts preserved in oil, drained
12 stuffed green olives, halved
2 tablespoons capers in wine vinegar, drained
1 tablespoon chopped fresh Italian parsley
1 tablespoon chopped fresh oregano
DRESSING:
5 tablespoons extra virgin olive oil
2 tablespoons white wine vinegar
1 teaspoon Dijon mustard
1 teaspoon finely grated lemon peel
1 teaspoon clear honey
Salt and freshly ground black pepper

Arrange eggs on a serving plate with artichokes and olives. Sprinkle over capers and herbs.

To make dressing, mix ingredients together in a small bowl until evenly blended or shake together in a screw-top jar. Pour over salad and serve at once.

Serves 4-6.

Note: Artichoke hearts preserved in oil are similar, but far superior, to canned artichoke hearts. Find them at Italian delicatessens.

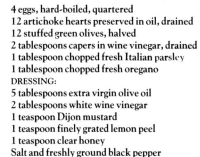

AUBERGINES & TOMATO SAUCE

8-10 small aubergines (eggplants), total weight about
450 g (1 lb)
Salt
6 tablespoons extra virgin olive oil
1 shallot, finely chopped
2 cloves garlic, crushed
450 g (1 lb) tomatoes, skinned and finely chopped
2 sprigs fresh oregano
85 ml (3 fl oz/⅓ cup) red wine
1 tablespoon sun-dried tomato paste
1 tablespoon chopped fresh Italian parsley
Salt and freshly ground black pepper
Fresh herb sprigs to garnish

Meanwhile, heat 2 tablespoons of the oil in a small saucepan, add shallot and garlic and cook for 3-4 minutes to soften. Stir in tomatoes and oregano and cook for a further minute.

Leaving stalk end intact, slice the aubergines (eggplants) lengthwise 3 or 4 times so they can be flattened out to give a 'fanned' appearance.

Add wine and sun-dried tomato paste and bring to the boil. Lower the heat, cover and simmer for 10 minutes, stirring frequently, until vegetables are tender. Discard oregano then stir in parsley and season with salt and freshly ground black pepper.

Place in a shallow dish. Sprinkle with salt and leave to stand for 25-30 minutes. Rinse thoroughly to remove salt. Drain and pat dry using absorbent kitchen paper; set aside. Preheat grill.

Arrange aubergines (eggplants), on a baking sheet. Press each aubergine (eggplant) to fan out slices. Brush with remaining 4 tablespoons olive oil and cook under the hot grill for 5-6 minutes, turning once, until tender and beginning to brown. Serve immediately with hot sauce.

Serves 4.

—AUBERGINE & OLIVE SALAD—

450 g (1 lb) aubergines (eggplant), diced
Salt
10 tablespoons light olive oil
2 onions, chopped
1 clove garlic, chopped
4 sticks celery, sliced
2 small courgettes (zucchini), sliced
1 tablespoon chopped fresh rosemary
400 g (14 oz) can chopped plum tomatoes
1 tablespoon sun-dried tomato paste
2 teaspoons sugar
85 ml (3 fl oz/⅓ cup) red wine vinegar
175 g (6 oz) stoned mixed olives, halved
2 tablespoons capers in wine vinegar, drained
Salt and freshly ground black pepper
Fresh Italian parsley sprigs to garnish

Put aubergines (eggplant) in a colander; sprinkle with plenty of salt and leave to drain for 30-40 minutes. Rinse thoroughly to remove salt, drain and pat dry on absorbent kitchen paper. Heat 4 tablespoons of the oil, in a frying pan over a high heat. Add aubergines (eggplant) and fry for 4-5 minutes until evenly browned. Transfer aubergines (eggplants) to absorbent kitchen paper. Heat remaining oil in a large frying pan. Stir in onions and garlic and fry gently for 5 minutes to soften.

Add celery, courgettes (zucchini) and rosemary and cook for a further 5 minutes. Stir in tomatoes, sun-dried tomato paste, sugar and vinegar and cook, stirring frequently, for 10 minutes until vinegar has evaporated. Transfer to a serving dish. Set aside to cool, then add reserved aubergines (eggplant), olives and capers. Season with salt and freshly ground black pepper and toss well. Chill. Serve garnished with Italian parsley sprigs.

Serves 4-6.

—CANNELINI BEAN PASTE—

225 g (8 oz) dried cannelini beans, soaked overnight and drained
½ teaspoon hot red pepper flakes
2 teaspoons tomato purée (paste)
2 sprigs fresh rosemary
25 g (1 oz) butter
2 tablespoons extra virgin olive oil
1 clove garlic, finely chopped
1 tablespoon finely chopped fresh oregano
175-225 ml (6-8 fl oz/¾ cup - 1 cup) hot chicken stock
Juice 1 lemon
Salt and freshly ground black pepper
Toasted crusty bread, vegetable sticks or warmed crusty bread to serve
Fresh rosemary sprigs to garnish

Put beans in a saucepan with 900 ml (32 fl oz/4 cups) water, the red pepper flakes, tomato purée (paste) and rosemary sprigs. Bring to the boil then lower the heat, cover and simmer gently for 2 hours until most of the water has been absorbed and beans are very tender. Discard rosemary. In a food processor or blender, purée beans and remaining liquid until very smooth.

Heat butter and oil in a medium saucepan. Add garlic and oregano. Cook for 2 minutes. Stir in bean purée and hot stock and cook gently for 10-12 minutes, stirring frequently, until mixture is very thick. Remove from heat, stir in lemon juice and season with salt and freshly ground black pepper. Serve either hot spread on toasted crusty bread or cold with fresh vegetable sticks or warmed crusty bread. Garnish with rosemary sprigs.

Serves 6.

MARINATED MUSHROOMS

MARINATED OLIVES

450 g (1 lb) mixed mushrooms such as button cups,
    ceps (porcini), oyster, shiitake
300 ml (10 fl oz/1¼ cups) white wine vinegar
2 small fresh red chillies, halved lengthwise and seeded
Grated peel 1 lemon
2 bay leaves
2 teaspoons coriander seeds
1 teaspoon cumin seeds
1 teaspoon black peppercorns
3 cloves garlic, sliced
300 ml (10 fl oz/1¼ cups) olive oil

450 g (1 lb) black olives
1 fresh red chilli, seeded and chopped
3 cloves garlic, chopped
2 sprigs fresh thyme
2 teaspoons dill seeds, lightly crushed
Salt and freshly ground black pepper
Olive oil to cover
2 tablespoons chopped fresh dill

Using a small sharp knife make a lengthwise
slit through to the stone of each olive.

Thickly slice any large mushrooms, otherwise
leave whole. Put vinegar, chillies, lemon
peel, bay leaves, coriander, and cumin seeds,
peppercorns and 300 ml (10 fl oz/1¼ cups)
water in a medium saucepan. Bring to the
boil then add the mushrooms and cook for
7-8 minutes until tender. Drain away liquid
and spread mushrooms and flavourings on
absorbent kitchen paper to dry.

Put olives in a bowl with chilli, garlic, thyme
and dill seeds. Season with salt and freshly
ground black pepper. Pour over olive oil to
just cover, cover bowl and leave in refrigerator for 3-14 days.

Fill a 550 ml (1 pint/2½ cups) preserving jar
with boiling water. Pour out water and put jar
in a warm oven to dry; then leave to cool. Fill
with mushroom mixture and the garlic
slivers. Pour oil over to cover mushrooms
completely. Seal tightly and leave in a cool
place to marinate for at least 5 days before
serving. Will keep for about 3 months. After
opening, store in refrigerator.

*Makes sufficient to fill a 550 ml (1 pint/2½ cup)
jar.*

Drain olives; reserve oil for cooking or salad
dressings. Discard thyme sprigs. Serve olives
sprinkled with chopped fresh dill.

Serves 6.

PRAWN VOL-AU-VENTS

ANCHOVY BEIGNETS

30 g (1 oz) butter
2 tablespoons plain flour
315 ml (10 fl oz / 1 ¼ cups) milk
60 g (2 oz) peeled prawns, chopped
squeeze of lemon juice
2 teaspoons snipped fresh chives
pinch of cayenne pepper
1 teaspoon paprika
salt
36 cocktail vol-au-vent (oyster) cases

Melt the butter in a saucepan, add the flour
and stir well over a low heat for 2 minutes.
Remove from heat and add the milk all
at once.

Return to the heat and stir until the sauce
boils and thickens. Remove from the heat.
Add the prawns, lemon juice, chives, cayenne and paprika. Season to taste with salt.
Cool the mixture slightly.

60 g (2 oz) butter
125 ml (4 fl oz / ½ cup) water
60 g (2 oz / ½ cup) plain flour
4 canned anchovy fillets, drained and mashed
2 eggs
30 g (1 oz) slivered almonds
vegetable oil for deep-frying

Cut the butter into cubes and put into a
saucepan with the water. Heat until butter
melts, then bring to the boil.

Add the flour all at once and stir for about
1 minute, until the paste leaves the side of
the saucepan. Cool. Transfer to a bowl. Beat
in the anchovy fillets and eggs, 1 at a time,
until mixture is glossy. Stir in the slivered
almonds.

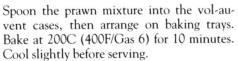

Spoon the prawn mixture into the vol-au-
vent cases, then arrange on baking trays.
Bake at 200C (400F/Gas 6) for 10 minutes.
Cool slightly before serving.

Makes 36.

Heat the oil in a medium saucepan. When
hot drop a few teaspoonfuls of the anchovy
mixture into the oil. Cook a few at a time for
about 5 minutes, until golden. Remove with
a slotted spoon and drain on absorbent paper.
Repeat until all the batter is used. Serve hot.

Makes 12 to 15.

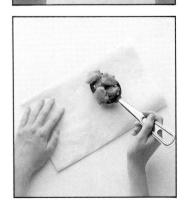

DEEP FRIED SMALL FISH

MUSSEL & FENNEL SALAD

225 g (8 oz) small fish such as anchovies, whitebait,
    baby sardines
55 g (2 oz/½ cup) plain (all-purpose) flour
2 teaspoons finely chopped fresh Italian parsley
Salt and freshly ground black pepper
Vegetable oil for deep frying
Lemon slices to serve

Rinse fish thoroughly, drain and pat dry on
absorbent kitchen paper.

1.5 kg (3 lb) mussels in their shells
1 clove garlic, chopped
1 fennel bulb
1 small onion, sliced
85 ml (3 fl oz/⅓ cup) extra virgin olive oil
Juice 1 lemon
Salt and freshly ground black pepper

Scrub mussels, rinse thoroughly and remove
beards. Discard any that do not close when
tapped firmly. Put in a large saucepan with
garlic and 4 tablespoons water. Cover and
cook on a high heat for about 5 minutes until
shells open.

Put flour, parsley, salt and freshly ground
black pepper into a plastic or paper bag and
shake to mix. Add fish in batches and shake
gently until coated.

Drain and reserve 2 tablespoons cooking
liquor. Discard any unopened mussels. Leave
remainder to cool completely. Trim fennel,
reserving feathery tops to garnish. Cut bulb
into matchsticks. Place in a serving dish with
onion.

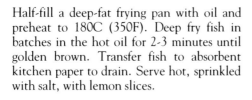

Half-fill a deep-fat frying pan with oil and
preheat to 180C (350F). Deep fry fish in
batches in the hot oil for 2-3 minutes until
golden brown. Transfer fish to absorbent
kitchen paper to drain. Serve hot, sprinkled
with salt, with lemon slices.

Serves 4.

Note: The fish are eaten whole so it is necessary to choose only those which are small
enough not to require cleaning.

Remove and discard shells from most of the
mussels leaving 12-16 intact. Add all of
the mussels to serving dish with the reserved
cooking liquor. Season with salt and ground
black pepper. Trickle olive oil and lemon
juice over and toss to mix. Serve sprinkled
with reserved fennel.

Serves 4-6.

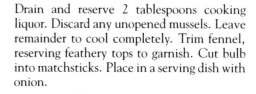

STUFFED GRILLED MUSSELS

MINTED SEAFOOD SALAD

1.5 kg (3 lb) large mussels in their shells
70 ml (2½ fl oz/⅓ cup) dry white wine
25 g (1 oz/½ cup) fresh white breadcrumbs
85 ml (3 fl oz/⅓ cup) olive oil
3 tablespoons chopped fresh Italian parsley
1 tablespoon finely chopped fresh oregano
2 cloves garlic, crushed
Salt and freshly ground black pepper
Lemon slices and fresh Italian parsley to garnish

Scrub mussels and remove beards. Discard any that do not close when tapped firmly. Put in a large saucepan with white wine.

150 ml (5 fl oz/⅔ cup) dry white wine
1 shallot, chopped
5 whole black peppercorns
400 g (1 lb) shelled scallops, fresh or frozen and thawed
450 g (1 lb) cooked large prawns
4 sticks celery
2 medium carrots
About 16 whole fresh mint leaves
½ teaspoon finely grated lemon peel
DRESSING:
Juice 2 lemons
115 ml (4 fl oz/½ cup) extra virgin olive oil
1 tablespoon white wine vinegar
2 tablespoons chopped fresh Italian parsley
Salt and freshly ground black pepper

Cover and boil for 4-5 minutes, until shells open. Strain, reserving liquid. Discard any unopened mussels. Remove and discard half of each shell, leaving mussels on remaining halves. In a bowl, mix together breadcrumbs, half of the olive oil, herbs, and garlic. If bread is still dry add a little of the reserved mussel juice to moisten.

Put white wine, shallot, peppercorns and 70 ml (2½ fl oz/⅓ cup) water in a shallow saucepan. Heat until boiling then add scallops. Lower the heat and poach for 5-6 minutes, until scallops are just firm and opaque. Using a slotted spoon transfer scallops to absorbent kitchen paper to drain and cool. Discard cooking liquid. Slice scallops in half horizontally. Put in a serving dish. Peel prawns and add to dish.

Preheat grill. Divide breadcrumb mixture between mussels on their shells and arrange on baking sheets. Sprinkle the remaining olive oil over and cook under the hot grill for 1-2 minutes until crumb mixture is crisp and golden. Serve hot garnished with lemon slices and parsley leaves.

Serves 4-6.

Cut celery and carrots into thin matchsticks and add to seafood with mint leaves and lemon peel. Toss lightly to mix. To make dressing mix ingredients together in a small bowl until evenly blended or put in a screwtop jar and shake until blended. Pour over salad and toss. Cover and refrigerate for 30 minutes before serving.

Serves 4-6.

SQUID SALAD

450 g (1 lb) small or medium squid
300 ml (10 fl oz/1¼ cups) dry white wine
1 shallot, chopped
Strip lemon peel
1 clove garlic, chopped
1 red onion, chopped
4 tablespoons chopped fresh mixed herbs such as basil, tarragon and Italian parsley
DRESSING:
5 tablespoons extra virgin olive oil
2 tablespoons lemon juice
1 teaspoon balsamic vinegar
½ teaspoon Dijon mustard
Salt and freshly ground black pepper
Fresh herb sprigs to garnish

Clean squid. If very small leave whole, otherwise slice flesh into rings. Put wine, shallot, lemon peel and garlic into a medium saucepan. Bring to the boil and cook for 1 minute. Add squid, in batches if necessary, and cook for 5-7 minutes until firm but still tender. Using a slotted spoon, remove to a serving dish and leave to cool.

Add onion and herbs to squid and toss to mix. To make dressing, mix ingredients together in a small bowl until evenly blended or shake together in a screw-top jar. Pour over salad and toss to mix. Chill for at least 30 minutes before serving garnished with fresh herb sprigs.

Serves 4.

SCALLOPS WITH GARLIC

12 large scallops, on the half shell
4 tablespoons extra virgin olive oil
2 cloves garlic, chopped
2 tablespoons chopped fresh Italian parsley
70 ml (2½ fl oz/⅓ cup) dry white wine
Juice 1 lemon
Salt and freshly ground black pepper
Lemon slices and fresh Italian parsley sprigs to garnish

Remove scallops from their shells and rinse under cold running water. Drain on absorbent kitchen paper. Clean 6 scallop shells thoroughly and set aside in a warm oven, for serving.

Heat oil in a frying pan. Add garlic and parsley and fry for 1 minute. Lower heat and stir in scallops. Season with salt and freshly ground black pepper, cover and cook for 5 minutes, stirring twice. Stir wine into pan, cover and continue to cook, for 3 minutes. Remove lid and cook on a higher heat for 4-5 minutes to reduce liquid by half. Remove from the heat.

Add lemon juice to pan and stir well. Adjust seasoning and divide scallops between reserved scallop shells. Divide cooking liquid between them. Serve immediately garnished with lemon slices and parsley sprigs.

Serves 4-6.

FRIED SARDINE FILLETS

700 g (1 ½ lb) small fresh sardines
2 eggs
225 g (8 oz/2 cups) dried white breadcrumbs
1 tablespoon finely chopped fresh oregano
1 tablespoon finely chopped fresh Italian parsley
Salt and freshly ground black pepper
Vegetable oil for deep frying
Lemon slices and fresh Italian parsley sprigs to serve

Remove heads from sardines and slit each fish along stomach side. Clean thoroughly. Lay each fish cut side down on a board. Press firmly along backbones to loosen then turn fish over and lift away bones.

Beat eggs in a shallow dish. In a separate shallow dish mix breadcrumbs, herbs and seasoning.

Half-fill a deep-fat frying pan with oil and preheat to 180C (350F). Dip each sardine fillet into beaten egg then into breadcrumb mixture to coat. Deep fry sardines, two at a time, in the hot oil for about 4 minutes until golden brown. Using a slotted spoon, transfer to absorbent kitchen paper to drain. Serve at once with lemon slices and Italian parsley sprigs.

Serves 4.

DEEP FRIED SQUID & PRAWNS

225 g (8 oz) medium squid
350 g (12 oz) large prawns, in the shell
55 g (2 oz/½ cup) plain (all purpose) flour
1 teaspoon salt
Vegetable oil for deep frying
Lemon wedges and fresh Italian parsley sprigs to serve

Clean and prepare squid. Slice body parts into rings. Shell prawns and devein.

Put flour in a shallow dish. Roll squid and prawns in the seasoned flour to coat.

Half-fill a deep-fat frying pan with oil and preheat to 180C (350F). Add a few pieces of fish at a time to hot oil and deep fry for about 3 minutes until golden. Using a slotted spoon transfer to absorbent kitchen paper. Serve hot with lemon wedges and Italian parsley sprigs.

Serves 4.

MIXED SEAFOOD SALAD

150 ml (5 fl oz/²⁄₃ cup) dry white wine
Juice ½ lemon
1 shallot, chopped
8 sprigs fresh Italian parsley, separated into stalks and
  leaves
1 clove garlic, chopped
700 g (1½ lb) prepared raw seafood such as squid,
  clams and mussels and large prawns in their shells,
  shelled scallops
200 ml (7 fl oz/scant cup) prepared mayonnaise
½ teaspoon finely grated lemon peel
Salt and freshly ground black pepper
1 head lettuce, separated into leaves
Lemon slices to garnish

Chop parsley leaves with remaining clove garlic.

Put wine, 150 ml (5 fl oz/²⁄₃ cup) water, the lemon juice, shallot, parsley stalks and 1 clove garlic in a large saucepan. Bring to the boil and boil for 1 minute. Add seafood in succession according to length of cooking time of each type, starting with those that need longest cooking – allow 15 minutes for squid, 5-6 minutes for prawns, 4-5 for scallops, 2-3 for mussels and clams. Using a slotted spoon, transfer cooked pieces to a large bowl.

Put parsley and garlic in a bowl and stir in mayonnaise and lemon peel. Season with salt and freshly ground black pepper. Transfer to a serving bowl.

Strain cooking liquor into bowl and allow to cool. Cover and put in refrigerator for at least 1 hour.

Arrange lettuce leaves as a bed on a serving plate. Drain seafood and pile into centre of plate. Season and garnish with lemon slices. Serve mayonnaise separately.

Serves 4-6.

BAGNA CAUDA

2 × 50 g (1¾ oz) cans anchovy fillets, drained and
    roughly chopped
300 ml (10 fl oz/1¼ cups) whipping cream
3 cloves garlic, crushed
55 g (2 oz) unsalted butter, diced
Fresh Italian parsley sprigs to garnish
TO SERVE:
Cubes crusty bread
Grissini
Vegetables for dipping, such as fennel, celery, peppers
    (capsicum), radishes, chicory, broccoli

Put anchovies in a small saucepan with cream
and garlic. Bring to the boil then lower the
heat and simmer gently, uncovered and
stirring occasionally, for 12-15 minutes until
smooth and thickened.

Stir in butter. Transfer to a serving dish and
garnish with parsley. Serve with cubes of
bread, grissini and vegetables for dipping.

Serves 4.

Note: Traditionally, the serving dish is kept
hot at the table like a fondue, over a candle or
spirit burner.

TUNA STUFFED TOMATOES

8 medium firm but ripe tomatoes
1 red onion, finely chopped
1 clove garlic, crushed
2 tablespoons chopped fresh Italian parsley
2 tablespoons chopped basil
3 tablespoons extra virgin olive oil
2 teaspoons red wine vinegar
200 g (7 oz) can tuna in olive oil, drained and flaked
Salt and freshly ground black pepper
Fresh basil leaves to garnish
Mixed salad leaves to serve

Slice tops off tomatoes and discard. Using a
teaspoon, carefully scoop out seeds from
tomatoes. Set tomatoes aside and discard
seeds.

In a bowl mix together onion, garlic, parsley,
basil, olive oil and vinegar. Add tuna and
seasoning and stir lightly to mix. Divide
between tomatoes. Put in refrigerator for at
least 1 hour. Garnish with basil leaves and
serve with mixed salad leaves.

Serves 4.

PRAWNS WITH MELON

DRESSED CRAB

12 cooked Mediterranean prawns
1 small Charentais melon
1 small Galia or Ogen melon
Juice 1 small lemon
Salt and freshly ground black pepper
Fresh mint leaves, to garnish

Peel prawns leaving tail tips on, if desired.

2 cooked crabs each weighing about 1 kg (2 lb)
4 tablespoons extra virgin olive oil
Juice 1 lemon
Salt and freshly ground black pepper
TO GARNISH:
1 red pepper (capsicum) packed in wine vinegar,
    drained
Lemon slices
Fresh Italian parsley or fennel sprigs

Remove large claws and legs from crabs. Crack open. Remove flesh. Flake into a bowl.

Cut melons into thin wedges and remove skins.

Prise open one body and remove any white meat and all the brown meat from body shell, discarding mouth part, grey stomach sacks and feathery gills. Add all the crabmeat to the bowl. Scrub shell clean. Repeat with other crab.

Arrange prawns and the two varieties of melon on a serving plate or individual plates and sprinkle with lemon juice. Season with salt and freshly ground black pepper. Serve garnished with fresh mint leaves.

Serves 4-6.

Sprinkle olive oil and lemon juice over crabmeat and season with salt and freshly ground black pepper. Mix together lightly with a fork. Pile meat back into crab shells and serve cold garnished with strips of red pepper (capsicum), lemon slices and parsley or fennel sprigs.

Serves 4.

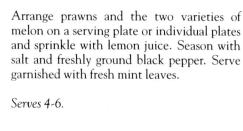

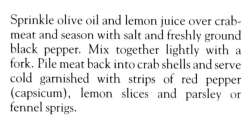

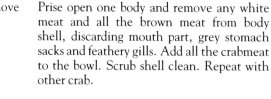

MARINATED FISH

450 g (1 lb) very fresh red mullet or sardines, cleaned
1 clove garlic, chopped
Juice 2 lemons
½ red onion, finely chopped
¼ teaspoon hot red pepper flakes
4 tablespoons extra virgin olive oil
Salt and freshly ground black pepper
1 teaspoon chopped fresh Italian parsley and Italian
    parsley sprigs to garnish

Remove heads, tails, fins and backbones of fish. Wash fillets and pat dry. Arrange in one layer in a shallow dish.

Sprinkle with chopped garlic and pour over juice of 1½ lemons. Cover and refrigerate for 24 hours, turning fish once.

Drain fish thoroughly and arrange in a serving dish. Sprinkle with red onion and hot pepper flakes. Pour over remaining lemon juice and olive oil and season with salt and freshly ground black pepper. Serve garnished with chopped Italian parsley and Italian parsley sprigs.

Serves 4.

Note: It is important to use fish that is very fresh as it is 'cooked' only by the acid in the lemon juice.

TUNA SALAD

3 small carrots, thickly sliced
225 g (8 oz) potato, diced
200 g (7 oz) can tuna in olive oil, drained and chopped
50 g (1¾ oz) can anchovy fillets in oil, drained and
    chopped
About 12 stoned black olives, halved
2 tablespoons capers in wine vinegar, drained
2 eggs, hard-boiled, quartered
4 tablespoons extra virgin olive oil
Juice 1 small lemon
1 clove garlic, crushed
Salt and freshly ground black pepper
1 tablespoon chopped fresh Italian parsley and Italian
    parsley sprigs to garnish

Cook carrots in a saucepan of boiling salted water for 4 minutes until tender. Cook potato in a separate pan of boiling salted water for about 7 minutes until tender. Drain and refresh both vegetables under cold running water. Drain and allow to cool completely.

Put carrots and potatoes with tuna, anchovies, olives, capers and eggs into a large serving dish. Mix olive oil, lemon juice, garlic and salt and pepper together in a small bowl or put in a screw-top jar and shake until blended. Pour over salad and toss lightly to mix then garnish with chopped Italian parsley and Italian parsley sprigs.

Serves 4.

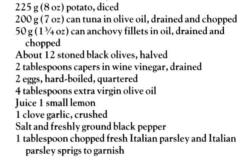

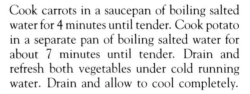

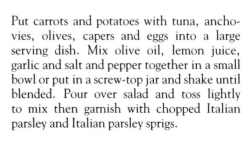

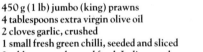

CRAB & PRAWN TOASTS

225 g (8 oz) white crabmeat, flaked
115 g (4 oz) peeled prawns
2 teaspoons lemon juice
25 g (1 oz) butter
25 g (1 oz/¼ cup) plain (all-purpose) flour
300 ml (10 fl oz/1¼ cups) milk
2 tablespoons marsala
½ teaspoon Dijon mustard
1 tablespoon chopped fresh Italian parsley
2 tablespoons double (thick) cream
Salt and freshly ground black pepper
4 slices toasted crusty white bread to serve
Fresh Italian parsley sprigs and lemon slices to garnish

Put crabmeat, prawns and lemon juice in a small bowl and mix lightly. Melt butter in a small saucepan. Stir in flour and cook, stirring, for 1 minute. Remove from heat then gradually whisk in milk. Return to heat and bring to the boil, stirring constantly. Lower heat and simmer for 5 minutes, stirring frequently.

Stir in marsala and mustard, then remove from heat and lightly fold in parsley, cream and crabmeat mixture. Season with salt and freshly ground black pepper. Spoon over slices of hot toasted crusty bread and serve immediately garnished with Italian parsley sprigs and lemon slices.

Serves 4.

FRIED KING PRAWNS

450 g (1 lb) jumbo (king) prawns
4 tablespoons extra virgin olive oil
2 cloves garlic, crushed
1 small fresh green chilli, seeded and sliced
2 tablespoons chopped fresh Italian parsley
1-2 tablespoons Sambuca or other anise liqueur
Salt and freshly ground black pepper
Lemon wedges to garnish

Remove heads and fine legs from prawns and discard.

Heat oil in a large frying pan. Add garlic, chilli and prawns and fry quickly for 2-3 minutes, until prawns turn bright pink.

Stir in parsley and Sambuca and season with salt and freshly ground black pepper. Serve at once garnished with lemon wedges.

Serves 4.

GRILLED BUTTERFLY PRAWNS

450 g (1 lb) jumbo (king) prawns
Juice 1 lemon
5 tablespoons extra virgin olive oil
½ clove garlic, crushed
2 tablespoon sun-dried tomato paste
Pinch cayenne pepper
1 tablespoon chopped fresh basil
Salt and freshly ground black pepper
Fresh basil leaves to garnish

Remove heads and fine legs from prawns.
Using sharp scissors cut prawns lengthwise
almost in half, leaving tail end intact.

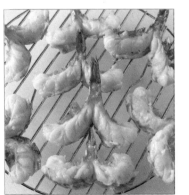

Place in a shallow dish and pour over half of
the lemon juice and 2 tablespoons of the olive
oil. Stir in garlic. Leave for at least 30
minutes. Preheat grill. Arrange prawns in
one layer on a rack and cook under the hot
grill for about 3 minutes until prawns have
curled or 'butterflied' and are bright pink.

In a small bowl, mix together remaining
lemon juice and 3 tablespoons olive oil, the
sun-dried tomato paste, cayenne, basil, salt
and freshly ground black pepper. Either
spoon over prawns or serve separately for
dipping. Garnish prawns with basil sprigs.

Serves 4.

TUNA PÂTÉ

45 g (1½ oz) butter
4 spring onions (scallions), white part only, chopped
2 sticks celery, finely chopped
200 g (7 oz) can tuna in brine, drained
2 tomatoes, skinned, seeded and chopped
2 tablespoon prepared mayonnaise
1 teaspoon lemon juice
1 teaspoon white wine vinegar
Salt and freshly ground black pepper
Chopped fresh Italian parsley and stoned green olives
   to garnish
Crusty bread or toast to serve

Melt butter in a small frying pan. Add spring
onions (scallions) and celery and cook gently
for 5 minutes, to soften. Leave to cool.

Put cooled spring onions (scallions) mixture
in a food processor or blender with remaining
ingredients and process until fairly smooth.
Transfer to a serving dish, cover and refrigerate for at least 30 minutes. Garnish with
chopped Italian parsley and stoned green
olives and serve with crusty bread or toast.

Serves 4-6.

SEAFOOD PÂTÉ

500 g (1 lb) white fish fillets
500 g (1 lb) raw prawns
90 g (3 oz) butter
6 spring onions, chopped
250 g (8 oz) scallops (optional)
1 clove garlic, crushed
2 tablespoons Cognac or brandy
125 ml (4 fl oz / ½ cup) single cream
1 tablespoon lemon juice
1 teaspoon paprika
good pinch of cayenne pepper
lemon slices, fresh dill sprigs and peeled cooked
    prawns, to serve

To remove the skin from the fish, place the fish, skin down and use a sharp knife to separate flesh, pulling skin from side to side. Cut the fish into chunks. Peel and de-vein the prawns.

Melt the butter in a frying pan and gently sauté the spring onions for 2 minutes. Add the fish, prawns, scallops (if used) and garlic. Cook, turning until the prawns turn pink and the fish flakes.

Warm the Cognac, ignite and pour over the fish mixture. When the flames subside, add the cream. Stir in the lemon juice, paprika and cayenne. Cool. Put the mixture into a food processor and blend. Turn the mixture into one large or several small serving dishes, cover and chill until firm. Garnish with lemon slices, sprigs of dill and prawns. Serve with crackers, Melba toast or celery.

Serves 10.

SEAFOOD TOASTS

2 slices white bread
250 g (8 oz) raw prawns
250 g (8 oz) white fish fillets
2 eggs
1 tablespoon ginger wine or dry sherry
1 tablespoon soy sauce
½ teaspoon salt
1 tablespoon cornflour
fresh parsley sprigs (optional)
vegetable oil for deep-frying

Trim crusts thickly from bread so each square measures about 7 cm (2¾ in). Cut each diagonally into halves.

Peel and de-vein the prawns. Remove any bones and skin from the fish. Put prawns and fish into a food processor with 1 egg, the ginger wine, soy sauce, salt and cornflour. Blend to a smooth paste. Spread evenly on the pieces of bread.

Beat the remaining egg and brush over the spread seafood. Press a sprig of parsley on top of each. Heat the oil in a frying pan. When hot add the seafood-topped bread, a few pieces at a time. Turn triangles occasionally until golden all over. Drain and repeat until all are cooked. Serve hot or warm.

Makes 24.

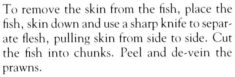

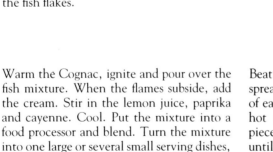

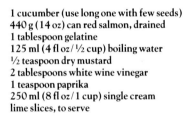

TARAMASALATA

SALMON MOUSSE

2 thick slices of crusty bread, weighing about
   180 g (6 oz)
125 g (4 oz) tarama (salted grey mullet roe)
1 clove garlic, crushed
1 tablespoon grated onion
1 egg yolk
2-3 tablespoons lemon juice
125 ml (4 fl oz / ½ cup) olive oil
black olive and fresh chives, to garnish
crusty bread, to serve

Remove the crusts from the bread. Cover in cold water and soak for 10 minutes. Squeeze out the water.

Crumb the bread in a food processor. Remove. Place the tarama in the processor, add the garlic and onion and process until thoroughly mixed. Gradually add the bread-crumbs until the mixture is smooth. Blend in the egg yolk and 1 tablespoon of the lemon juice.

With the processor on, gradually pour in the olive oil, mixing until very creamy. Add more lemon juice to taste. Cover and chill. Garnish with a black olive and chives. Serve with crusty bread for dipping.

Serves 10.

Note: Tarama is the salted roe from grey mullet and is available from many deli-catessens, and larger supermarkets.

1 cucumber (use long one with few seeds)
440 g (14 oz) can red salmon, drained
1 tablespoon gelatine
125 ml (4 fl oz / ½ cup) boiling water
½ teaspoon dry mustard
2 tablespoons white wine vinegar
1 teaspoon paprika
250 ml (8 fl oz / 1 cup) single cream
lime slices, to serve

Trim the cucumber ends and cut lengthwise into thin slices using a mandolin or cutter. Line a long narrow 500 ml (16 fl oz / 2 cup) loaf tin with the slices.

Mash salmon with a fork and remove any bones. Put the salmon flesh into a food processor and mix well. Dissolve the gelatine in the boiling water and pour over the salmon. Add the mustard, vinegar and paprika and blend well together until smooth.

Add the cream and blend until just mixed. Pour into the lined tin and chill until set. Turn out of the mould, cut into slices and serve on thin crispbreads or biscuits with lime slices.

Serves 4 to 6.

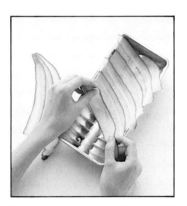

SALMON PUFFS

CRISPY ALMOND SQUID

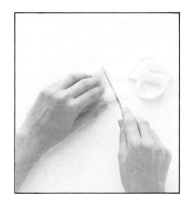

60 g (2 oz / ½ cup) plain flour
125 ml (4 fl oz / ½ cup) water
60 g (2 oz) butter, diced
½ teaspoon salt
30 g (1 oz) Cheddar cheese, finely grated
2 eggs
250 g (8 oz) can red salmon, drained
2 tablespoons mayonnaise
1 tablespoon sliced stuffed olives
red salmon roe or caviar, to garnish

500 g (1 lb) cleaned calamari bodies (hoods)
60 g (2 oz / ½ cup) plain flour
salt and pepper
2 eggs, beaten
125 g (4 oz / 1 cup) dry breadcrumbs
60 g (2 oz / ½ cup) finely chopped unblanched almonds
vegetable oil for deep frying
lemon slices and fresh parsley sprigs, to serve

Slice the calamari into rings.

Sift the flour on to a sheet of greaseproof paper. Heat the water and butter with salt until boiling.

Add the flour all at once to the water and stir over a low heat for about 1 minute, until the mixture leaves the sides of the pan and forms a ball. Remove from the heat, add the cheese and spread out on a plate to cool. Beat in the eggs, 1 at a time, until well blended.

Season the flour with salt and pepper. Roll the calamari rings in the flour, then dip into the beaten egg. Mix the breadcrumbs with the almonds on a sheet of greaseproof paper. Roll the calamari rings in the breadcrumb mixture, making sure they are well coated. Chill on flat trays until ready to fry.

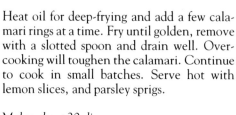

When well combined, put small teaspoonfuls of the mixture on to a greased baking tray. Bake at 200C (400F/Gas 6) for 20 minutes, until puffed and golden. Cool. Combine the salmon with the mayonnaise and olives. Split the puffs and fill with the salmon mixture. Add a small amount of roe or caviar and serve immediately.

Serves 4 to 6.

Heat oil for deep-frying and add a few calamari rings at a time. Fry until golden, remove with a slotted spoon and drain well. Overcooking will toughen the calamari. Continue to cook in small batches. Serve hot with lemon slices, and parsley sprigs.

Makes about 20 slices.

CAVIAR MOUSSE

HERB & GARLIC MUSSELS

250 g (8 oz) black caviar
2 teaspoons gelatine
125 ml (4 fl oz / ½ cup) boiling water
300 ml (10 fl oz) carton thick sour cream
3 spring onions, finely chopped
hard-boiled eggs and fresh herbs (optional), to garnish

The caviar mousse is best not made more than 24 hours before serving. Put the caviar in a bowl. Dissolve the gelatine in the boiling water and stir into the caviar.

Divide the caviar mixture between four small moulds or pour into one large mould. Chill until set. Meanwhile, combine the sour cream with the spring onions. Cover and chill until needed.

Unmould the caviar shapes by dipping the moulds into hot water and turning upside down on to a serving platter. Garnish with cut-out shapes of hard-boiled egg whites, sieved yolks, and sprigs of fresh herbs. Serve with the sour cream sauce and lemon wedges.

Makes 4 small moulds or 1 large mould.

1 kg (2 lb) unshelled mussels
500 ml (16 fl oz / 2 cups) water
125 g (4 oz) butter
2 cloves garlic, crushed
2 tablespoons chopped fresh parsley
1 tablespoon snipped fresh chives
1 tablespoon chopped fresh dill

Scrub the mussels well, removing the beards. Cover with cold water and soak for several hours. Discard any mussels with broken shells. Drain.

Bring the water to the boil in a frying pan. Add a layer of mussels and remove them once they open. Add more mussels as the cooked ones are removed. Discard any that do not open. Lift off the top shell of each mussel and discard. Beat the butter with the remaining ingredients.

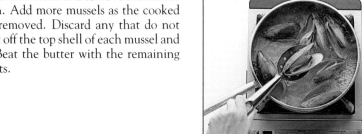

Spread the herb butter over each of the mussels. Chill until ready to cook. Place under a hot grill until tops colour. Serve hot.

Makes about 30, depending on the size of the mussels.

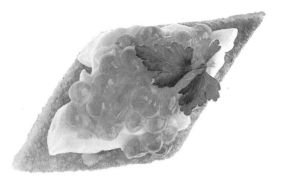

CROÛTONS WITH ROE

10 slices white bread
2 tablespoons vegetable oil
30 g (1 oz) butter
1-2 teaspoons bottled hot horseradish
125 ml (4 fl oz / ½ cup) thick sour cream
3 tablespoons red salmon roe
fresh parsley sprig, optional

To make the croûtons, cut shapes out of sliced bread. Use shaped cutters for hearts and cut diamonds with a knife. Trimmings can be used for making breadcrumbs.

Heat oil and butter in a small frying pan. When hot, fry the bread pieces until they are golden, turning to colour both sides. Drain on absorbent paper and cool. The croûtons may be prepared ahead of time and stored in an airtight container.

Stir the horseradish into the sour cream, adding more to taste if preferred. Just before serving spoon the sour cream on to the croûtons and top with the salmon roe. Garnish with parsley sprigs, if desired.

Makes 20.

OPEN SALMON SANDWICHES

6 thin slices black, rye or sweet and sour bread
60 g (2 oz) butter, at room temperature
1 crisp, curly endive or lettuce, torn into small pieces
250 g (8 oz) thinly sliced smoked salmon
fresh dill sprigs and lemon twists, to garnish

Cut the bread into rounds using a biscuit cutter.

Spread the rounds liberally with butter. Top each round with the curly endive or lettuce.

Fold the salmon and arrange on top. Garnish with a dill sprig and a lemon twist. A dab of sour cream flavoured with chopped dill and chopped capers can be put on top, if desired. Serve immediately or chill briefly until ready to serve.

Makes 6.

PARMA HAM ROULADES

YAKITORI

60 g (2 oz) Ricotta cheese
60 g (2 oz) Stilton cheese
1 tablespoon thick sour cream
12 very thin slices Parma ham (prosciutto) or coppa or
    ham deluxe
1 pear, apple or fresh fig

250 g (8 oz) skinned chicken breasts (fillets)
6 spring onions
2 tablespoons sake
2 tablespoons light soy sauce
½ teaspoon grated fresh root ginger
2 teaspoons sugar

Blend both cheeses with the sour cream. Spread evenly on the thin slices of Parma ham (prosciutto), taking the mixture almost to the edges.

Cut the chicken pieces into small cubes.

Peel the pear, cut into quarters and remove the core, then thinly slice. Place a piece of pear on each cheese-topped slice of prosciutto.

Wash and trim the spring onions and cut them into 4 cm (1½ in) lengths, using some of the green tops. Thread the chicken cubes and spring onions alternately on to 6 bamboo skewers.

Roll up the ham. Place on a dish, cover and chill until ready to serve. Apples or fresh figs, when in season, may be used instead of the pear. Peel and slice the figs before using.

Makes 12.

Heat the sake and add the remaining ingredients. Place the skewers on the grill tray and cover the exposed ends of the skewers with a sheet of foil. Brush the sake mixture over chicken and onions. Grill until the chicken is cooked (about 6 minutes), brushing with the marinade and turning occasionally. Serve hot.

Makes 6.

STUFFED ONIONS

4 large onions
225 g (8 oz) minced veal
2 slices unsmoked streaky bacon, finely chopped
45 g (1½ oz/⅓ cup) provolone cheese, grated
1-2 cloves garlic, crushed
1 tablespoon sun-dried tomato paste
1 tablespoon finely chopped fresh Italian parsley
1 tablespoon chopped fresh oregano
1 small egg, beaten
Salt and freshly ground black pepper
Fresh Italian parsley or oregano sprigs to garnish

Preheat oven to 200C (400F/Gas 6). Grease an ovenproof dish. Put onions in a large saucepan, cover with water and bring to the boil. Cook for 25-30 minutes until just tender. Drain and allow to cool slightly. Cut onions in half horizontally. Using a teaspoon, remove centres to leave shells with about 3 layers. Use pieces of the centres to cover any holes in the bases; discard remainder.

Mix together remaining ingredients in a bowl. Divide between onion shells and arrange in the ovenproof dish. Bake in the preheated oven for 40-45 minutes until filling is cooked through. Serve hot garnished with Italian parsley or oregano sprigs.

Serves 4.

POLLO FRITTO

450 g (1 lb) chicken breast and thigh meat
3 tablespoons olive oil
Juice ½ lemon
1 clove garlic, crushed
55 g (2 oz/½ cup) plain (all-purpose) flour
2 eggs, beaten
225 g (8 oz/2 cups) dried white breadcrumbs
1 teaspoon paprika
Salt and freshly ground black pepper
Groundnut or light olive oil for deep frying
Lemon wedges to serve
Fresh Italian parsley leaves to garnish

Cut chicken into 5 cm (2 inch) pieces and place in a shallow dish. Add olive oil, lemon juice and garlic and stir well. Cover and leave for at least 1 hour. Put flour in a shallow dish. Put eggs in a separate shallow dish, and mix breadcrumbs, paprika and salt and pepper in a third. Drain chicken. Coat a few pieces at a time, first in the flour, then the egg, then in the seasoned breadcrumb mixture.

Half-fill a deep-fat frying pan with the oil and preheat to 180C (350F). Deep fry coated chicken pieces in batches in the hot oil for about 3 minutes, turning once until crisp and golden. Serve hot with lemon wedges. Garnished with Italian parsley leaves.

Serves 4.

BRESAOLA SALAD

VENETIAN CHICKEN SALAD

16 slices bresaola
Mixed salad leaves
4 large fresh basil leaves, shredded
Lemon slices to garnish
DRESSING:
3 tablespoons extra virgin olive oil
¼ teaspoon finely grated lemon peel
Juice ½ lemon
Salt and freshly ground black pepper

45 g (1½ oz/⅓ cup) sultanas or raisins
Juice 1 orange
55 g (2 oz)/⅓ cup) pine nuts
450 g (1 lb) cold cooked chicken, cut into strips
Small pinch ground cloves
85 ml (3 fl oz/⅓ cup) extra virgin olive oil
1 tablespoon white wine vinegar
1-2 teaspoons balsamic vinegar
Salt and freshly ground black pepper
Mixed salad leaves to serve

Heat sultanas or raisins and orange juice to boiling point in a small saucepan. Remove from heat. Leave for about 20 minutes. Drain and set aside fruit; discard liquid.

Arrange bresaola and salad leaves on individual serving plates or a large plate. Sprinkle over shredded basil leaves.

Put pine nuts in a small saucepan or frying pan, without oil, place over a medium heat and stir for 3 minutes until golden.

In a small bowl, mix together olive oil, lemon peel and juice and spoon over dish. Season with salt and freshly ground pepper. Garnish with lemon slices.

Serves 4.

Put pine nuts and other ingredients except the salad leaves, in a bowl and toss well to mix. Leave to stand for 30 minutes. Serve with mixed salad leaves.

Serves 4-6.

PARMA HAM WITH FIGS

BRESAOLA & CHEESE ROLLS

12 paper-thin slices Parma ham
4-6 ripe figs
Fresh Italian parsley leaves or mint sprigs to garnish

115 g (4 oz) dolcelatte cheese
55 g (2 oz) mascarpone cheese
Salt and freshly ground black pepper
12 thin slices bresaola
Salad leaves
Juice 1 lemon
3 tablespoons extra virgin olive oil
Lemon slices to garnish

In a small bowl mix together dolcelatte and mascarpone cheeses until well blended. Season with salt and freshly ground black pepper.

Arrange Parma ham slices on a serving platter or individual plates.

Lay bresaola slices on a board. Divide cheese mixture between slices and roll up.

Halve or quarter figs lengthwise and arrange beside ham. Serve garnished with parsley leaves or mint sprigs.

Serves 4.

Arrange salad leaves on a serving plate or individual plates and place bresaola rolls on top. Sprinkle with lemon juice and extra virgin olive oil and a little more black pepper. Serve garnished with lemon slices.

Serves 4.

CARPACCIO

300 g (10 oz) piece beef fillet
85 g (3 oz) piece Parmesan, thinly sliced
225 g (8 oz) button mushrooms, thinly sliced
Leaves from 8 sprigs fresh Italian parsley
DRESSING:
115 ml (4 fl oz/½ cup) extra virgin olive oil
Juice 2 lemons
1 clove garlic, chopped
Salt and freshly ground black pepper

Put beef in freezer for 30 minutes. Using a very sharp knife, cut beef into wafer thin slices.

Lay beef slices in centre of a large serving plate and arrange Parmesan slices, mushrooms and parsley around edge.

To make dressing, whisk together all dressing ingredients in a small bowl or put in a screw-top jar and shake until thoroughly blended. Pour over beef, Parmesan, mushrooms and parsley.

Serves 6.

ITALIAN MEAT PLATTER

115 g (4 oz) mixed thinly sliced salamis
55 g (2 oz) mortadella, thinly sliced
55 g (2 oz) prosciutto or coppa, sliced
55 g (2 oz) bresaola
2 large pickled cucumbers
1 small bunch radishes, trimmed
175 g (6 oz) cherry tomatoes
115 g (6 oz) black or green olives
Salad leaves
DRESSING:
5 tablespoons extra virgin olive oil
2 tablespoons lemon juice
1 tablespoon red wine vinegar
1 teaspoon Dijon mustard
Salt and freshly ground black pepper

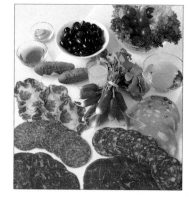

Arrange meats and sausages on a large plate. Slice pickled cucumbers thinly on the diagonal and add to plate with radishes, tomatoes, olives and salad leaves.

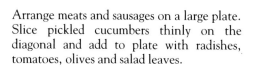

To make dressing mix ingredients together in a small bowl until evenly blended and serve with meats.

Serves 6-8.

Note: Selection of meats can be varied to include your favourite Italian sausages, salamis etc. Serve with crusty bread, bread rolls or bread sticks.

VEAL & SPINACH TERRINE

450 g (1 lb) fresh spinach
450 g (1 lb) minced veal
115 g (4 oz) lean unsmoked bacon, finely chopped
85 g (3 oz/¾ cup) provolone cheese, grated
25 g (1 oz/½ cup) fresh white breadcrumbs
1 tablespoon chopped fresh Italian parsley
2 eggs, beaten
Salt and freshly ground black pepper
Fresh Italian parsley sprigs to garnish

PORK & LIVER PÂTÉ

350 g (12 oz) unsmoked streaky bacon slices
225 g (8 oz) pork shoulder, chopped
225 g (8 oz) pigs liver, chopped
225 g (8 oz) pork sausagemeat
1 small onion, chopped
2 cloves garlic, chopped
1 tablespoons chopped fresh thyme
1 tablespoon chopped fresh oregano
3 tablespoons marsala
Salt and freshly ground black pepper
Fresh herb sprigs to garnish

Preheat oven to 170C (325F/Gas 3). Grease a
450 g (1 lb) loaf tin. Lay bacon slices on a
board and stretch using the back of a knife.

Preheat oven to 160C (320F/Gas 3). Grease
and line base of a 1 kg (2 lb) terrine or loaf
tin. Rinse spinach thoroughly; do not dry.
Cook in a large saucepan without additional
water for about 2 minutes until wilted. Tip
into a sieve and press out excess water using a
wooden spoon. Chop finely.

Line the loaf tin with the bacon slices,
reserving a few slices to cover top. Place pork
shoulder in a blender or food processor and
process until finely chopped. Add remaining
ingredients and process briefly until well
blended but not smooth. Put pork mixture
into prepared loaf tin, smooth top and cover
with remaining bacon. Cover tightly with
foil.

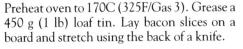

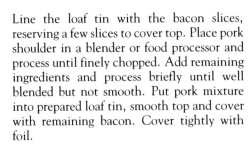

In a large mixing bowl mix spinach with
remaining ingredients. Spoon into the
terrine or loaf tin. Cover with foil and cook in
the preheated oven for 1-1¼ hours until
firm. Remove from oven but cool in tin. Turn
out and serve sliced, garnished with Italian
parsley sprigs.

Serves 6.

Place loaf tin in a roasting tin half-filled with
boiling water. Cook in the preheated oven for
1½-1¾ hours until firm. Remove foil. Cover
pâté with greaseproof paper then put a plate
or board and a heavy weight on top; leave
until cold. Chill overnight. Serve sliced,
garnished with fresh herb sprigs.

Serves 6-8.

HAM CRESCENTS

125 g (4 oz) full fat soft (cream) cheese
125 g (4 oz) butter
125 g (4 oz / 1 cup) plain flour
250 g (8 oz) cooked ham, finely minced
1 tablespoon prepared hot English mustard
2 tablespoons thick sour cream
1 egg, beaten, to glaze

Cream together the cheese and butter in a bowl until light. Work in the flour to form a dough. Knead lightly on a lightly floured surface. Wrap and chill.

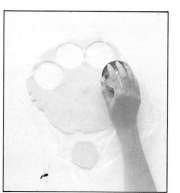

Mix the ham, mustard and sour cream together in a bowl. Chill until ready to use. Roll out the pastry on a well-floured surface. (In a hot weather, it is easier to roll between 2 sheets of cling film/plastic wrap). Cut into rounds using a 7.5 cm (3 in) cutter.

Put a heaped teaspoon of ham mixture on each pastry round. Brush the pastry edge with egg and fold over, then press to seal. Fork the joined edges and glaze with the egg. Pierce each pastry with the point of a knife to allow steam to escape. Place on a baking tray and bake at 200C (400F/Gas 6) for 10 to 15 minutes, until golden. Serve hot.

Makes 20 to 24.

CHICKEN & GRAPE SALAD

450 g (1 lb) cold cooked chicken
115 g (4 oz/1¼ cups) walnut halves
115 g (4 oz) green seedless grapes, halved
16 stuffed green olives, sliced
3 spring onions (scallions), sliced
Salt and freshly ground black pepper
DRESSING:
150 ml (5 fl oz/⅔ cup) prepared mayonnaise
1 clove garlic, crushed
1 teaspoon paprika
2 tablespoons chopped fresh Italian parsley
Few drops hot pepper sauce
2 tablespoons milk
1 head lettuce, separated into leaves

Cut chicken into thin strips and place in a bowl with walnuts, grapes, olives and spring onions (scallions). Season with salt and freshly ground black pepper.

To make dressing mix ingredients together in a small bowl until evenly blended. Pour over salad and toss gently to mix. Arrange lettuce on a serving plate. Pile chicken salad in centre and serve at once.

Serves 4-6.

ITALIAN SAUSAGES & LENTILS

350 g (12 oz/2 cups) green lentils
2 tablespoons extra virgin olive oil
55 g (2 oz) unsmoked streaky bacon, chopped
1 onion, finely chopped
2 cloves garlic, crushed
2 sticks celery, finely chopped
Salt and freshly ground black pepper
4-6 spicy fresh Italian pork sausages
Chopped fresh Italian parsley and Italian parsley sprigs,
   to garnish

Put lentils in a bowl, cover with water and leave to soak for 2 hours. Drain.

Heat 1 tablespoon of the oil in a large sauce-pan or sauté pan. Add bacon, onion, garlic and celery and cook for 3-4 minutes until beginning to brown. Add lentils and water to just cover. Bring to the boil, then simmer for 25 minutes until lentils are tender, adding a little more water if necessary. Season with salt and freshly ground black pepper.

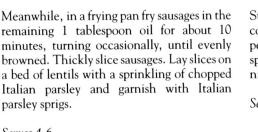

Meanwhile, in a frying pan fry sausages in the remaining 1 tablespoon oil for about 10 minutes, turning occasionally, until evenly browned. Thickly slice sausages. Lay slices on a bed of lentils with a sprinkling of chopped Italian parsley and garnish with Italian parsley sprigs.

Serves 4-6.

SAUTÉED LAMB'S KIDNEYS

12 lambs kidneys
25 g (1 oz) butter
1 tablespoon olive oil
2 cloves garlic, crushed
1 small onion, finely chopped
1 teaspoon wholegrain mustard
4 tablespoons marsala
Salt and freshly ground black pepper
Hot toasted bread to serve
Chopped fresh Italian parsley and Italian parsley sprigs
   to garnish

Remove and discard thin membrane surrounding kidneys. Cut each in half. Using kitchen scissors, cut out white cores; discard.

Heat butter and oil in a frying pan. Add garlic and onion and sauté for 3 minutes until just soft. Add kidneys and cook over a high heat, stirring, for 2-3 minutes until browned but still tender.

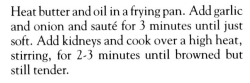

Stir mustard and marsala into the pan and cook with salt and freshly ground black pepper. Serve on hot toasted bread and sprinkle with chopped Italian parsley. Garnish with Italian parsley sprigs.

Serves 4-6.

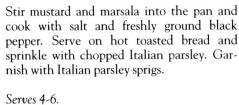

FRITTO MISTO

85 g (3 oz/¾ cup) plain (all-purpose) flour
Salt and freshly ground black pepper
2 eggs, beaten
225 g (8 oz/2 cups) dry white breadcrumbs
4 lamb's kidneys, halved and cored
225 g (8 oz) calves liver, cut into strips
1 small aubergine (eggplant) sliced
225 g (8 oz) spicy fresh Italian sausages, cut into bite-size pieces
2 medium courgettes (zucchini), thickly sliced
Sunflower or groundnut oil for frying
Fresh Italian parsley sprigs to garnish

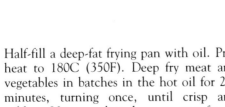

Put flour and seasoning into a shallow dish. Put eggs in a separate dish and breadcrumbs in a third. Dip kidneys, liver, aubergine (eggplant) and courgettes (zucchini) first in flour then in egg and finally in breadcrumbs to coat evenly.

Half-fill a deep-fat frying pan with oil. Preheat to 180C (350F). Deep fry meat and vegetables in batches in the hot oil for 2-4 minutes, turning once, until crisp and golden. Using a slotted spoon transfer to absorbent kitchen paper to drain. Serve hot garnished with fresh Italian parsley sprigs.

Serves 6-8.

CHICKEN LIVER TOASTS

3 tablespoons olive oil
1 stick celery, finely chopped
2 cloves garlic, crushed
225 g (8 oz) chicken livers, chopped
1 teaspoon chopped fresh sage
4 tablespoons marsala
2 anchovy fillets canned in oil, drained
1 tablespoon capers in wine vinegar, drained
Freshly ground black pepper
1 medium stick French bread
Capers and sage leaves to garnish

Preheat oven to 190C (375F/Gas 5). Heat oil in a large frying pan. Add celery and garlic and cook for 2 minutes to soften.

Add chicken livers and fry over a high heat, stirring occasionally, for about 3 minutes until crisp and brown on the outside but just pink inside. Using a wooden spoon, stir in sage and marsala, scraping up all the cooking juices; transfer to a blender or food processor and add anchovy fillets and capers. Season with freshly ground black pepper and process until fairly smooth. To keep hot transfer to a warmed plate, cover and put over a saucepan of hot water.

Cut bread diagonally into thick slices and lay on a baking tray. Bake in the oven for 6-7 minutes, until golden. Serve chicken liver paste on the baked bread, garnishing each piece with capers and a sage leaf.

Serves 6-8.

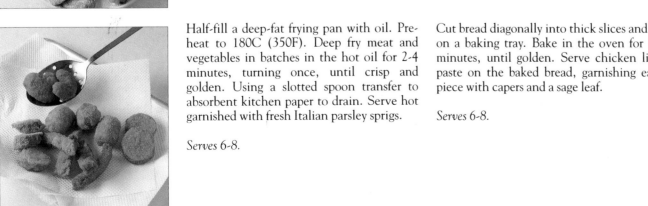

CHICKEN WITH GREEN SAUCE

BRANDIED LIVER PÂTÉ

450 g (1 lb) cold cooked chicken
Mixed salad leaves
SAUCE:
175 g (6 oz) fresh Italian parsley
8 sprigs fresh basil
50 g (1¾ oz) can anchovy fillets in oil, drained
1 shallot, chopped
2 cloves garlic, crushed
3 tablespoons white wine vinegar
1 teaspoon Dijon mustard
15 g (½ oz/¼ cup) fresh white breadcrumbs
115 ml (4 fl oz/½ cup) extra virgin olive oil
Freshly ground black pepper

225 g (8 oz) calves liver
225 g (8 oz) chicken livers
115 g (4 oz) butter
Sprig fresh rosemary
1 bay leaf
5 tablespoons brandy
Salt and freshly ground black pepper
Fresh rosemary sprigs to garnish

Clean livers and discard any veins or stringy parts. Dice calves liver, and cut chicken livers in half.

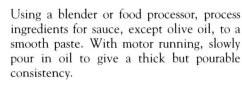

Using a blender or food processor, process ingredients for sauce, except olive oil, to a smooth paste. With motor running, slowly pour in oil to give a thick but pourable consistency.

Melt 25 g (1 oz) of the butter in a large frying pan; add rosemary, bay leaf and chicken livers and cook over a high heat for 3 minutes until crisp on the outside but still pink inside. Remove to a food processor or blender, and set aside. Add calves liver to pan and cook over a high heat for about 3 minutes. Add to chicken livers. Using a wooden spoon, stir 2 tablespoons of the brandy into pan, scraping up the cooking juices then allow to sizzle.

Slice the chicken and arrange with salad leaves on a serving plate or individual plates. Pour sauce over and around chicken.

Serves 4-6.

Discard herbs from pan then pour cooking juices into the blender or food processor. Process until smooth. Transfer to a bowl; leave to cool. Beat remaining butter and brandy into liver mixture. Season with salt and freshly ground black pepper and transfer to a serving bowl. Put in refrigerator for a few hours until firm. Serve garnished with rosemary sprigs.

Serves 4.

CHINESE DUMPLINGS

125 g (4oz) won ton wrappers
250 g (8 oz) can bamboo shoots
4 spring onions
250 g (8 oz) lean minced pork
½ teaspoon grated fresh root ginger
1 teaspoon salt
1 egg white
2 teaspoons soy sauce
plum or chilli sauce for dipping

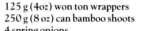

Won ton wrappers can be purchased from Asian food shops. Finely chop the bamboo shoots and the spring onions.

Combine these vegetables with the pork, ginger, salt, egg white and soy sauce. Mix together well. Put one heaped teaspoonful of this mixture on each won ton square, keeping the unused squares covered with a damp piece of absorbent paper.

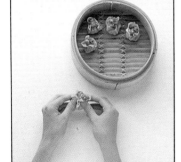

Squeeze the pastry around the filling to resemble a money bag. Place without the dumplings touching each other, in an oiled bamboo steaming basket. Steam over boiling water for 20 minutes. Serve hot with plum sauce or chilli for dipping.

Makes about 20.

SPICY PORK ROLLS

250 g (8 oz) pork fillet
6 or 7 spring onions
1 clove garlic, crushed
1 tablespoon dark soy sauce
1 tablespoon honey
1 tablespoon oil
1 tablespoon hoi sin sauce
1 teaspoon grated fresh root ginger

Trim any fat and sinew from the pork and cut the fillets crosswise into 20 thin slices.

Gently pound the meat with a knife to flatten. Trim the spring onions and cut into short lengths. Combine the remaining ingredients in a shallow ovenproof dish and mix well.

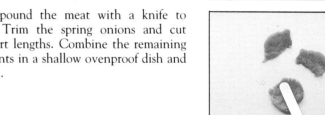

Roll each slice of meat around a piece of spring onion. The moisture in the meat will keep the rolls intact. Place the pork rolls in the soy mixture. If preparing ahead of serving time, cover and chill. Cook at 200C (400F/ Gas 6) for 10 to 15 minutes, basting with the sauce as they cook. Serve hot or warm.

Makes 20.

SALAMI CRESCENTS

2 sheets frozen puff pastry or 375 g (12 oz) frozen block
   puff pastry
2 tablespoons sour cream
1 teaspoon hot prepared mustard
8 slices mettwurst salami
8 slices Emmenthal (Swiss) cheese
1 egg, beaten, to glaze

Cut each sheet of pastry into quarters so each
square measures 17.5cm (7 in). If using a
block of puff pastry, roll out thinly and cut
eight 17.5 cm (7 in) squares.

Mix the sour cream and mustard and spread
evenly over the pastry squares, taking the
mixture almost to the edges of the pastry. Cut
the salami and cheese slices into halves.
Place on the pastry and cut each square of
pastry diagonally into halves, then into
quarters.

Starting from the wide side of each triangle,
roll up the filling in the pastry. Place on
greased baking sheets and bend the pastries
gently into crescent shapes. Brush with the
beaten egg. Bake at 200C (400F/Gas 6) for
10 to 15 minutes or until golden. Serve hot.

Makes 32.

LIVERWURST CANAPÉS

2 small loaves crusty French bread
3 tablespoons olive oil
2 tablespoons melted butter
1 small clove garlic, crushed
250 g (8 oz) smoked liverwurst
6 thin slices Emmenthal (Swiss) cheese, cut into
   squares
6-12 pickled dill cucumbers

Choose the narrow French loaves that will
cut into small rounds. Slice bread into 1 cm
(½ in) thick rounds.

Mix the oil and butter with the garlic. Brush
bread slices on both sides with butter
mixture. Place in one layer in a shallow
ovenproof dish and cook at 200C (400F/Gas
6) for 10 minutes, until golden and crispy on
the edges.

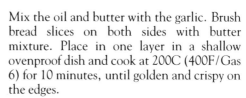

Mix the liverwurst until it softens and spread
evenly on each slice of bread. Top each with
a piece of cheese. Return to the oven for 5 to
10 minutes, until the cheese melts. Serve hot
with a piece of dill pickle on each.

Makes about 24.

SATAY SAUSAGE ROLLS

LIVERWURST BALLS

1 onion, finely chopped
1 tablespoon vegetable oil
1 tablespoon dark soy sauce
2 teaspoons lemon juice
2 cloves garlic, crushed
1 teaspoon hot chilli sauce
750 g (1½ lb) sausage-meat
3 eggs
2 x 375 g (12 oz) packets frozen puff pastry

Gently cook the onion in the oil over a low heat. Add soy sauce, lemon juice, garlic and chilli sauce.

Add the sausage-meat and 2 of the eggs to the onion mixture. Mix all well together. Roll out half the pastry on a lightly floured surface to 20 x 25 cm (8 x 10 in) rectangle. Cut lengthwise into 2 strips. Repeat with the other packet of pastry.

Pile sausage filling down the centre of each pastry strip. Beat the remaining egg. Brush edges of the pastry with the beaten egg. Fold pastry over and join to form a roll. Slash the top of the pastry and cut each roll into 4 cm (1½ in) lengths. Put rolls on baking sheets and bake at 200C (400F/Gas 6) until golden, about 20 minutes. Serve hot with a spicy sauce.

Makes 40.

2 rashers bacon, rind removed
1 small onion, finely chopped
250 g (8 oz) liverwurst
2 tablespoons brandy or Grand Marnier
1 large bunch of fresh parsley, finely chopped
shredded orange rind and nuts, to garnish

Finely dice the bacon. Fry bacon over a low heat, stirring until beginning to crisp. Remove the bacon. Add the onion to the pan and fry in the bacon fat over a low heat until transparent.

Put bacon, onion and liverwurst into a bowl. Warm the brandy or Grand Marnier, ignite and pour over the liverwurst. Mix together well. Chill to firm.

Put the chopped parsley on a sheet of grease-proof paper. Take heaped teaspoonfuls of the liverwurst mixture and roll into balls. Roll the balls in the parsley. Chill balls until ready to serve. If using brandy, a nut may garnish each ball. If using Grand Marnier, garnish with finely shredded orange rind.

Makes 12 to 15 balls.

BARBECUED CSABAI

4 csabai sausages (not the csabai salami which is much harder)

This appetiser makes an ideal start to a barbecue because not only is the taste delicious, but the flavour from the sausages penetrates the meats which are cooked later. The sausage can be grilled or fried on the oven. Cut the csabai into finger lengths and peel.

Split each piece of csabai lengthwise into halves. Cover and refrigerate until ready to cook.

Prepare the barbecue in advance so the coals are glowing. Grease the grid lightly with oil and place the csabai, cut side down, on the barbecue. Alternatively, use a frying pan over a moderate heat. Cook until coloured, turn and cook the other side. Cut into chunks and serve hot.

Makes about 50 pieces.

PIROSHKI WITH THYME

60 g (2 oz) fresh (compressed) yeast
2 tablespoons sugar
315 ml (10 fl oz / 1¼ cups) lukewarm milk
375 g (12 oz / 3 cups) plain flour
salt and pepper
180 g (6 oz) butter, melted
3 large onions, chopped
250 g (8 oz) bacon
1 egg, beaten to glaze
2 tablespoons fresh thyme leaves

Cream yeast with the sugar. Stir in the milk.

In a large bowl, mix flour and 2 teaspoons salt and make a well in the centre. Pour the yeast mixture and 125 g (4 oz) melted butter into the centre. Beat well for 3 minutes to form a smooth batter. Cover with cling film (plastic wrap) and leave in a warm place for 1 hour or until double in bulk. Gently sauté onions in remaining butter until golden. Cool. Chop bacon finely and add to the onions with 1 teaspoon pepper and the thyme.

Knead dough lightly, then divide into 35 to 40 portions. Wrap a teaspoon of the bacon filling in each portion of dough. Prove in a warm place on greased trays for 15 minutes. Brush with egg. Bake at 230C (450F/Gas 8) for 10 to 15 minutes.

Makes 35 to 40.

CHICKEN & SAUSAGE ROLLS

RUMAKI

500 g (1 lb) skinned chicken breasts (fillets)
salt and pepper
2 or 3 peperoni sausages
12 green beans, topped and tailed
6 sheets filo pastry
125 g (4 oz) butter, melted
mango chutney, if desired

Split the chicken breasts. Place a sheet of cling film (plastic wrap) over the breasts and beat them out thinly. Season with salt and pepper.

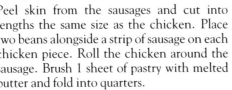

Peel skin from the sausages and cut into lengths the same size as the chicken. Place two beans alongside a strip of sausage on each chicken piece. Roll the chicken around the sausage. Brush 1 sheet of pastry with melted butter and fold into quarters.

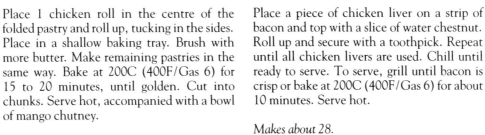

Place 1 chicken roll in the centre of the folded pastry and roll up, tucking in the sides. Place in a shallow baking tray. Brush with more butter. Make remaining pastries in the same way. Bake at 200C (400F/Gas 6) for 15 to 20 minutes, until golden. Cut into chunks. Serve hot, accompanied with a bowl of mango chutney.

Makes about 30.

500 g (1 lb) chicken livers
2 tablespoons vegetable oil
1 tablespoon soy sauce
1 tablespoon dry sherry
squeeze of lemon juice
1 clove garlic, crushed
10 canned water chestnuts, drained and sliced
about 12 bacon rashers

Halve the livers, removing connective tissue and any dark spots. Heat the oil in a frying pan and gently cook the livers, 1 layer at a time, turning constantly, until they change colour.

Remove from the heat. Add soy, sherry, lemon juice and garlic. Mix well. Cool. Remove bacon rinds. Cut each rasher into 2 or 3 pieces.

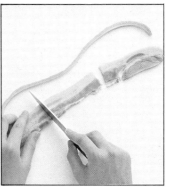

Place a piece of chicken liver on a strip of bacon and top with a slice of water chestnut. Roll up and secure with a toothpick. Repeat until all chicken livers are used. Chill until ready to serve. To serve, grill until bacon is crisp or bake at 200C (400F/Gas 6) for about 10 minutes. Serve hot.

Makes about 28.

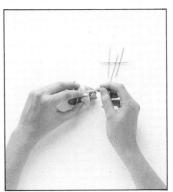

SMOKED BEEF TARTS

125 g (4 oz / 1 cup) plain flour
1 tablespoon grated fresh Parmesan cheese
60 g (2 oz) butter
1 egg, beaten
salt
440 g (14 oz) can artichoke hearts
125 g (4 oz) thinly sliced smoked beef
2 tablespoons sour cream
2 teaspoons chopped fresh dill sprigs
fresh dill sprigs and red pepper (capsicum) strips, to
    garnish

Sift flour, stir in cheese and rub in the butter.
Make a well in the centre, add the egg and
salt. Form into a dough and knead lightly.
Chill.

Roll out the pastry thinly between sheets of
cling film (plastic wrap) lightly dusted with
flour. Cut into rounds with a cutter and line
small greased tins. Chill. Prick well with a
fork and bake at 200 C (400F/Gas 6) for 10 to
15 minutes, until golden. Cool. Store in an
airtight container until ready to serve.

Drain the artichoke hearts well and rinse in
cold water. Cut into quarters or dice if the
artichokes are large. Cut the beef into strips
and roll each strip into a cylinder. Mix the
sour cream with the dill. Spoon a little sour
cream into each pastry case and top with
the artichoke and smoked beef. Serve
immediately. Garnish with dill sprigs and red
pepper strips.

Makes about 15.

CHICKEN SATAY

500 g (1 lb) skinned chicken breasts (fillets)
½ teaspoon sambal olek
1 teaspoon grated fresh root ginger
2 tablespoons lemon juice
3 tablespoons dark soy sauce
2 tablespoons honey
1 tablespoon peanut butter
125 ml (4 fl oz / ½ cup) water
cherries and fresh parsley sprigs, to garnish

Cut the chicken into 2.5 cm (1 in) cubes and
thread on to 15 bamboo skewers.

Put remaining ingredients, except the
cherries and parsley, into a large frying pan
or saucepan and heat, stirring well. Bring to
the boil, then lower heat and add chicken
skewers, cooking 1 layer at a time. Simmer
for 10 minutes, basting occasionally, then
remove chicken.

Repeat until all the skewers of chicken are
cooked, basting from time to time. Simmer
the sauce in the pan until it has reduced to
about 180 ml (6 fl oz / ¾ cup). Pour this
over the chicken. Chill. The skewers may be
garnished with cherries and fresh parsley
sprigs. Serve cold.

Makes 15.

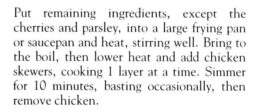

SAGE & ONION PINWHEELS

250 g (8 oz) full fat soft (cream) cheese
30 fresh sage leaves
3 tablespoons chopped spring onions
pepper

Soften the cheese and spread out on a sheet of foil to a 20 cm (8 in) square.

Lay the fresh sage leaves evenly over the cheese. If the sage is too dry and strong tasting, substitute chopped parsley, basil leaves or any other suitable fresh herb. Sprinkle with the spring onions and generously grind black pepper over the top.

Using the foil as a guide, roll up the cheese, making a tight log. Chill until firm or ready to serve. Cut into slices. Serve plain or on biscuits (crackers) or Melba toast.

Makes 18 to 20.

CHEESE-FILO PASTRIES

500 g (1 lb) feta cheese
3 tablespoons chopped fresh parsley
pepper
3 eggs, beaten
8 sheets filo pastry
125 g (4 oz) butter, melted

Crumble the cheese into a bowl. Mix together the parsley, pepper and beaten eggs. Stir into the cheese and mix together well.

Take 1 sheet of pastry and cut in half, keeping the remainder of the pastry covered with damp absorbent paper to prevent it drying out. Brush the pastry with melted butter and fold into quarters. Put a spoonful of the filling in the centre of each.

Squeeze the pastry around the filling to resemble a money bag (they may be cooked in buttered patty cake tins). Brush pastry with any remaining butter. Bake at 200C (400F/ Gas 6) for 20 to 25 minutes, until golden. Serve hot.

Makes 16.

EGGS & ANCHOVY MAYONNAISE

FRITTATA

85 g (3 oz) arugula or other lettuce leaves
4 eggs, hard-boiled, halved
1 teaspoon finely chopped fresh Italian parsley
1 teaspoon snipped fresh chives
DRESSING:
5 anchovy fillets canned in oil, drained
70 ml (2½ fl oz/⅓ cup) prepared mayonnaise
3-4 tablespoons milk
Freshly ground black pepper

1 large potato, about 300 g (10 oz)
25 g (1 oz) butter
2 tablespoons vegetable oil
1 small onion, chopped
1 red pepper (capsicum), seeded and diced
3 tablespoons chopped fresh herbs such as basil,
   oregano, mint, parsley, sage, thyme
4 eggs, beaten
Salt and freshly ground black pepper
Fresh herb sprigs or salad leaves to garnish

Cut potato into 2.5 cm (1 inch) pieces. Boil in salted water for 12-15 minutes until soft. Drain thoroughly then mash.

To make dressing, put anchovy fillets in a small bowl, mash with a fork then blend in mayonnaise, adding milk to give a smooth creamy consistency. Season with freshly ground black pepper.

Heat half of the butter and half of the oil in a large frying pan. Add onion and pepper (capsicum) and cook gently for 5 minutes to soften, but do not brown. Add to mashed potatoes with herbs and eggs. Season with salt and freshly ground black pepper.

Arrange salad leaves and eggs on a serving plate. Spoon anchovy mayonnaise over and around eggs and sprinkle with the herbs.

Serves 4.

Preheat grill. Heat remaining butter and oil in a large non-stick frying pan. Add potato mixture, spreading it evenly with a spatula. Cook over a medium heat for about 4 minutes until the bottom is set and lightly browned. Put under the grill until the top is set and golden. Serve hot or cold cut into wedges and garnished with fresh herb sprigs or with salad.

Serves 4-6.

PEPPERED PECORINO CHEESE

MOZZARELLA FRITTERS

450 g (1 lb) pecorino cheese
3 tablespoons black peppercorns, lightly crushed
1 teaspoon finely grated lemon peel, if desired
150 ml (5 fl oz/⅔ cup) extra virgin olive oil
Fresh Italian parsley sprigs to garnish

Remove rind from cheese and discard. Cut cheese into 2.5 cm (1 inch) cubes. Put into a shallow dish.

450 g (1 lb) mozzarella cheese
85 g (3 oz/¾ cup) plain (all-purpose) flour
1 teaspoon paprika
Salt and freshly ground black pepper
2 eggs, beaten
225 g (8 oz/2 cups) dried white breadcrumbs
Groundnut or vegetable oil for deep-frying
Fresh sage leaves to garnish

Cut mozzarella into 3.5 cm (1½ inch) cubes. Mix flour, paprika, salt and pepper in a shallow dish. Put eggs into a second dish and breadcrumbs in a third.

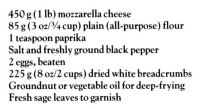

Sprinkle peppercorns, and peel, if using, over cheese. Pour over oil.

Coat cheese cubes lightly in the seasoned flour, dip into egg then into breadcrumbs to coat evenly. Repeat once more with egg and breadcrumbs.

Cover dish with foil and put in refrigerator for 2 hours, basting cheese occasionally. Remove from refrigerator 30 minutes before serving. Garnish with Italian parsley sprigs.

Serves 6-8.

Note: This dish can be kept covered in the refrigerator for up to 4 days but it is important to return it to room temperature 30 minutes before serving.

Half-fill a deep-fat frying pan with oil. Pre-heat to 180C (350F). Deep fry a few cheese cubes at a time in the hot oil for about 2 minutes until golden. Using a slotted spoon, transfer to absorbent kitchen paper to drain. Serve hot, garnished with sage leaves.

Serves 4-6.

EGG & WALNUT SALAD

ITALIAN CHEESE DIP

1 head lettuce
6 tomatoes, roughly chopped
½ red onion, thinly sliced
16 stoned black olives, halved
45 g (1½ oz/⅓ cup) walnut pieces
4 eggs, hard-boiled, quartered
1 tablespoon chopped fresh fennel
1 tablespoon snipped fresh chives
DRESSING:
3 tablespoons extra virgin olive oil
2 tablespoons walnut oil
2 tablespoons red wine vinegar
1 teaspoon wholegrain mustard
Pinch granulated sugar
Salt and freshly ground black pepper

½ red pepper (capsicum), seeded
½ yellow pepper (capsicum), seeded
55 g (2 oz) dolcelatte cheese
115 ml (4 fl oz/½ cup) mascarpone cheese
1 tablespoon lemon juice
2 small gherkins, finely chopped
Salt and freshly ground black pepper
Grissini and a selection of cooked and raw vegetables
    to serve

Tear lettuce into bite-sized pieces and put in a salad bowl with tomatoes, onion, olives, walnuts, eggs and herbs. Toss gently to mix.

Preheat grill. Cook peppers (capsicums), skin side up, under the hot grill for about 5-7 minutes, until skins are evenly blistered and charred. Transfer to a plastic bag for a few minutes then peel away and discard skins. Chop flesh finely and set aside.

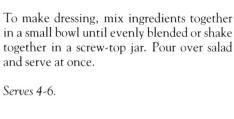

To make dressing, mix ingredients together in a small bowl until evenly blended or shake together in a screw-top jar. Pour over salad and serve at once.

Serves 4-6.

Put dolcelatte in a small bowl and mash with a fork. Stir in mascarpone and lemon juice until well blended then fold in chopped peppers (capsicums) and gherkins. Season with salt and freshly ground black pepper. Serve with grissini and a selection of cooked and raw vegetables.

Serves 4.

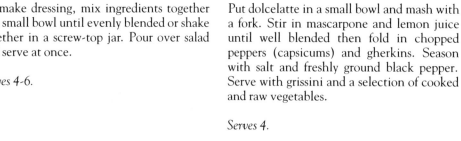

—POACHED EGGS FLORENTINE—

4 eggs
2 tablespoons white wine vinegar
25 g (1 oz) butter
350 g (12 oz) spinach leaves, finely shredded and rinsed
85 ml (3 fl oz/⅓ cup) double (thick) cream
2 tablespoons Dijon mustard
2 teaspoons chopped fresh Italian parsley
Salt and freshly ground black pepper
Hot buttered toast to serve
Paprika and fresh Italian parsley sprigs, to garnish

Preheat oven to a very low setting. To poach eggs, fill a large saucepan with water to a depth of 5 cm (2 inches). Add vinegar and bring to the boil. Lower the heat to a gentle simmer. Crack an egg onto a saucer and slide egg into pan. Repeat with another egg. Poach for about 3 minutes until cooked as desired. Using a slotted spoon, transfer to a warmed plate and put on lowest shelf in oven. Cook remaining 2 eggs, add to plate and keep warm in the oven.

Melt butter in a saucepan. Add spinach and cook, stirring, for 1-2 minutes until just wilted. Drain off any excess liquid then stir in cream, mustard and parsley. Season with salt and freshly ground black pepper. Serve the spinach and poached eggs accompanied by hot buttered toast. Sprinkle eggs with paprika and garnish with Italian parsley sprigs.

Serves 4.

—BAKED EGGS WITH RICOTTA—

25 g (1 oz) butter, melted
115 g (4 oz/½ cup) ricotta cheese
2 teaspoons snipped fresh chives
4 eggs
4 tablespoons double (thick) cream
Salt and freshly ground black pepper

Preheat oven to 180C (350F/Gas 4). Use butter to grease four individual heatproof dishes. Divide ricotta cheese between dishes, levelling surface with a teaspoon. Sprinkle chives over.

Break an egg into each dish and spoon cream over. Season with salt and freshly ground black pepper.

Place dishes in a shallow baking dish half-filled with warm water. Bake in the preheated oven for 10-12 minutes, until cooked as desired. Serve at once.

Serves 4.

FONDUTA

450 g (1 lb) fontina cheese, diced
300 ml (10 fl oz/1¼ cups) milk
55 g (2 oz) unsalted butter, melted
4 large egg yolks
Freshly ground black pepper
Fresh Italian parsley sprigs to garnish
Grissini, crusty bread or toast, for dipping

Place cheese and milk in a bowl. Leave for at least 2 hours to soften. Transfer to a double boiler or a heatproof bowl set over a pan of simmering water and heat until cheese melts and becomes stringy. Stir in butter and remove from heat.

Beat egg yolks in a small bowl then stir in a little of the hot cheese mixture. Pour back into remaining cheese mixture. Return to the heat and beat vigorously until smooth, creamy and thickened. Season with freshly ground black pepper.

Transfer to a serving dish (the dish is usually kept hot at table over a candle or spirit burner), garnish with Italian parsley sprigs and serve with grissini, crusty bread or toast for dipping.

Serves 6.

Note: If fontina cheese is not available a mixture of 225 g (8 oz) Gruyere and 225 g (8 oz) Edam is a good substitute.

STUFFED EGGS

6 eggs
85 g (3 oz/⅓ cup) soft cheese with garlic and herbs
3 tablespoons single (light) cream
1 tablespoon snipped fresh chives
Salt and freshly ground black pepper
Sliced, stoned black olives and chives, to garnish

Cook eggs in boiling water for 8-10 minutes until hard-boiled.

Drain eggs and place under cold running water until cool. Halve eggs lengthwise. Remove yolks from eggs and put in a bowl.

Mash yolks with a fork. Add cheese, cream and chives and mix well until smooth. Season with salt and freshly ground black pepper. Spoon or pipe into egg whites and serve garnished with sliced black olives and chives.

Serves 4-6.

MOZZARELLA SALAD

450 g (1 lb) mozzarella cheese
2 red onions, thinly sliced
1 tablespoon chopped fresh Italian parsley
1 tablespoon chopped fresh basil
1 tablespoon snipped fresh chives
1 teaspoon chopped fresh mint
50 g (1¾ oz) can anchovy fillets in oil, drained
Fresh Italian parsley sprigs to garnish
DRESSING:
5 tablespoons extra virgin olive oil
1 tablespoon white wine vinegar
1 teaspoon balsamic vinegar
½ clove garlic, crushed
Salt and freshly ground black pepper

Cut the mozzarella into slices. Arrange red onion on a large plate or individual plates. Lay mozzarella on top.

Sprinkle chopped herbs over mozzarella. To make dressing mix ingredients together in a small bowl or shake in a screw-top jar. Pour over salad. Arrange anchovy fillets on mozzarella and herbs in a lattice pattern, garnish with Italian parsley sprigs and serve at once.

Serves 4-6.

EGG & OLIVE SALAD

450 g (1 lb) small new potatoes
3 eggs, hard-boiled, halved or quartered
½ head cos (romaine) lettuce
18 stoned black olives, halved
Salt and freshly ground black pepper
85 ml (3 fl oz/⅓ cup) prepared mayonnaise
50 g (1¾ oz) can anchovy fillets in oil, drained
Paprika to garnish

Cook potatoes in boiling, salted water for 12-15 minutes, until tender. Drain and cool completely.

Halve or quarter potatoes and arrange with eggs, lettuce and olives on a serving plate or individual plates. Season with salt and freshly ground black pepper.

Spoon mayonnaise over salad and arrange anchovy fillets on top. Sprinkle with a little paprika. Serve chilled.

Serves 6.

MARINATED SOFT CHEESE

RICOTTA MOULDS

175 g (6 oz/¾ cup) ricotta cheese
175 g (6 oz/¾ cup) cream cheese
8 fresh Italian parsley sprigs, roughly chopped
8 fresh basil sprigs
1 tablespoon chopped fresh oregano
2 cloves garlic, chopped
¼ teaspoon hot red pepper flakes
Juice ½ lemon
10 black peppercorns, lightly crushed
150 ml (5 fl oz/⅔ cup) extra virgin olive oil
Fresh herb sprigs to garnish
Fresh vine leaves to serve, if desired

350 g (12 oz/1½ cups) ricotta cheese
1 tablespoon finely chopped fresh Italian parsley
1 tablespoon chopped fresh fennel
1 tablespoon snipped fresh chives
1 tablespoon gelatine
150 ml (5 fl oz/⅔ cups) prepared mayonnaise
Salt and freshly ground black pepper
Fresh chives, fennel and Italian parsley sprigs to garnish
PEPPER (CAPSICUM) SAUCE:
2 large red peppers (capsicums), grilled, deseeded and chopped, see page 100
3 tablespoons extra virgin olive oil
Few drops balsamic vinegar
Salt and freshly ground black pepper

In a mixing bowl, beat cheeses together with a wooden spoon. Divide into six and shape into balls or round patties. Arrange in one layer in an oiled shallow dish. Using a blender or food processor process remaining ingredients until fairly smooth.

In a bowl, mix together ricotta and herbs. Oil six 115-150 ml (4-5 fl oz/½ cup) moulds. In a small bowl, soak gelatine in 3 tablespoons cold water for 2 minutes. Place bowl over a saucepan of simmering water, stirring until dissolved. Cool slightly then stir into cheese mixture with mayonnaise and salt and freshly ground black pepper. Divide between moulds and chill until set.

Pour over cheeses. Cover dish with foil and put in refrigerator for 3 hours, basting cheeses occasionally. Remove from refrigerator 30 minutes before garnishing with herb sprigs and serving on a bed of fresh vine leaves, if desired.

Serves 6.

Note: If available 350 g (12 oz) stracchino or robiola can replace the cheeses in the recipe.

To make sauce, put peppers (capsicums) and oil in a food processor or blender and process until smooth. Add a few drops of balsamic vinegar and season with salt and freshly ground black pepper. Chill until required. To serve, turn out moulds onto individual plates; spoon the pepper (capsicum) sauce around the moulds and garnish with fresh herbs.

Serves 6.

STUFFED CHILLIES

12 large fresh red or green chillies
3 tablespoons extra virgin olive oil
1 tablespoon white wine vinegar
FILLING:
4 sun-dried tomatoes in oil, drained
150 g (5 oz/⅔ cup) mild soft goat's cheese
2 spring onions (scallions), white part only, finely
    chopped
2 teaspoon finely chopped fresh mint
1 teaspoon finely chopped fresh basil
Salt and freshly ground black pepper
Fresh mint leaves to garnish

Preheat grill. Cook chillies under the hot grill for 8-10 minutes, turning occasionally, until skins are evenly blistered and charred. Transfer to a plastic bag for a few minutes then peel away and discard skins. Make a slit along the length of each chilli. Carefully rinse off seeds under cold running water. Pat chillies dry with absorbent kitchen paper.

To make filling, finely chop sun-dried tomatoes and mix with remaining ingredients in a small bowl. Divide filling between chillies and arrange on a serving plate. Trickle over olive oil and vinegar. Put in refrigerator for at least 30 minutes before serving garnished with mint leaves.

Serves 4-6.

BROAD BEANS & GOATS CHEESE

4 tablespoons extra virgin olive oil
1 onion, chopped
1 kg (2 lbs) fresh broad beans, shelled, or 350 g (12 oz)
    frozen broad beans, thawed
1 tablespoon chopped fresh rosemary
Salt and freshly ground black pepper
2 heads chicory or 1 head radicchio
225 g (8 oz) goats cheese log, sliced
Fresh rosemary sprigs to garnish

Heat oil in a large frying pan, add onion and cook over a medium heat for about 10 minutes until soft and golden. Stir in beans and rosemary.

Add water to just cover beans and season with salt and freshly ground black pepper. Bring to the boil then cover and simmer for 12-15 minutes, stirring frequently, until beans are very tender and liquid is absorbed.

Preheat grill. Slice chicory or radicchio and stir into hot bean mixture. Lay goats cheese slices over the top. Put frying pan under the hot grill for 2-3 minutes until cheese is browned. Serve hot garnished with rosemary sprigs.

Serves 4-6.

CHEESE STRAWS

90 g (3 oz) butter
90 g (3 fl oz / ¾ cup) grated Cheddar cheese
125 g (4 oz / 1 cup) plain flour
1 teaspoon paprika
good pinch of cayenne pepper

Preheat the oven to 180C (350F/Gas 4). Cream the butter until light, then beat in the grated cheese.

Sift the flour and blend into the creamed butter mixture to make a dough. Divide the dough into balls, wrap each in cling film (plastic wrap) and chill until firm enough to roll. Roll out the dough between two sheets of cling film, dusted with a little flour. This makes the rolling of very short mixtures, such as this, much easier, particularly during hot weather.

Roll the dough to 3 mm (⅛ in) thick and cut into 10 cm (4 in) lengths, each 1 cm (½ in) wide. Place the cheese sticks on to baking trays and turn each end twice to give each stick 2 twists. Mix the paprika with the cayenne and, using a dry brush, dab the paprika on to the twists. Bake for 10 minutes.

Makes about 80.

BLUE CHEESE MUSHROOMS

12 to 14 button mushrooms
125 g (4 oz) blue cheese
125 g (4 oz) full fat soft (cream) cheese
1 tablespoon single cream
pecan nuts and fresh basil or parsley sprigs, to garnish

Wipe the mushrooms with a clean cloth dipped in cold water to which a few slices of lemon or a few drops of white vinegar has been added.

Cut out the stalks from the mushrooms (they can be used for cooking). Soften the cheeses and beat together until smooth, then beat in the cream. Put into a piping bag fitted with a star nozzle. If preparing ahead, place the mushrooms, covered, and the bag with the filling, in the refrigerator until just before serving.

Pipe the cheese mixture into the mushrooms. Top each with a nut and a basil or parsley sprig.

Makes 12 to 14.

— CHEESE & ONION PASTRIES —

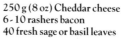

180 g (6 oz / 1 ½ cups) plain flour
½ teaspoon salt
125 ml (4 fl oz / ½ cup) cold water
24 spring onions
30 g (1 oz) butter
good pinch of cayenne pepper
125 g (4 oz) Gouda cheese, cut into 24 cubes
1 egg, beaten
vegetable oil for deep-frying

Sift the flour with the salt, then add the water to make a firm dough. Knead for 5 minutes, until smooth. Wrap and leave to rest for 30 minutes.

Chop the spring onions, including most of the green tops; there should be about 250 g (8 oz / 1 cup). Gently sauté onions in the butter until softened. Remove from the heat and add the cayenne pepper. Shape the dough into 24 balls and roll each out into a circle about 10 cm (4 in) wide.

Spoon a little spring onion mixture on to each pastry circle, top with a cheese cube and brush edges with the beaten egg. Fold pastry over the filling. Press edges together with a fork to seal. Deep-fry the pastries, a few at a time, in hot oil until golden. Drain and serve warm.

Makes 24.

— HERBED CHEESE BITES —

250 g (8 oz) Cheddar cheese
6 - 10 rashers bacon
40 fresh sage or basil leaves

Cut the cheese into 40 cubes. Trim the rind from the bacon and cut into lengths long enough to wrap around the cheese. Use bacon trimmings in other dishes.

Wrap a sage or basil leaf around each piece of cheese. Enclose in a piece of bacon and secure with wooden toothpicks. Place in a greased frying pan and cook over a moderate heat until bacon is crisp. Cool slightly and serve hot or warm.

Cheese and Peperoni Bites
Omit the sage or basil leaves and replace with a slice of peperoni salami. Follow the method above and serve in the same way.

Makes 40.

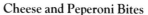
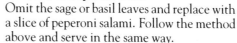

PEPPER CHEESE ROUNDS

250 g (8 oz) mature Cheddar cheese
250 g (8 oz) full fat soft (cream) cheese, at room
    temperature
60 ml (2 oz / ¼ cup) dry sherry
6 tablespoons coarsely cracked black peppercorns

Grate the Cheddar cheese into a bowl. Beat with the full fat soft cheese until well blended, then beat in the sherry.

Chill the mixture until firm and divide into four portions. Shape each into a log by rolling in a piece of cling film (plastic wrap). Alternatively, the cheese can be shaped into rounds.

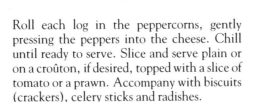

Roll each log in the peppercorns, gently pressing the peppers into the cheese. Chill until ready to serve. Slice and serve plain or on a croûton, if desired, topped with a slice of tomato or a prawn. Accompany with biscuits (crackers), celery sticks and radishes.

Makes 4 logs.

SESAME CHEESE BALLS

60 g (2 oz) sesame seeds
60 g (2 oz) pepitas or slivered almonds
250 g (8 oz) full fat soft (cream) cheese
2 tablespoons grated Parmesan cheese
2 teaspoons dried onion flakes
salt and pepper

Stir the sesame seeds in a dry frying pan over a moderate heat until they turn golden. Remove to a plate to cool. Put the pepitas or almonds on a baking tray and roast at 180C (350F/Gas 4) for 10 minutes. Cool.

Beat the cheeses and onion flakes well together. Season with salt and pepper to taste. Stir the sesame seeds into the cheese mixture and roll into 25 balls.

Place the toasted pepitas on a sheet of grease-proof paper and roll the cheese balls in the pepitas. Store in the refrigerator or a cool place until ready to serve.

Makes 25.

APRICOT CHEESE

250 g (8 oz) full fat soft (cream) cheese
90 g (3 oz) ready-to-eat dried apricots
60 g (2 oz) hazelnuts
4 tablespoons poppy seeds or toasted sesame seeds

Soften the cheese at room temperature and beat with a wooden spoon until smooth. Cut apricots into small chunks and add to the cheese.

Place the hazelnuts on a baking tray and place in an oven at 200C (400F/Gas 6) for 10 minutes. Remove from the oven and rub between several thicknesses of absorbent paper to remove skins. Return the nuts to the oven for a further 5 minutes or until golden. Chop roughly and mix with the cheese.

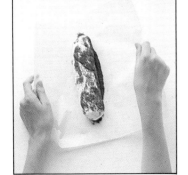

Form the cheese, on a sheet of greaseproof (wax) paper, in the shape of a 20 cm (8 in) long roll. Roll the log in the poppy seeds to coat it thoroughly. Chill until firm. Serve sliced on a board with biscuits (crackers) or apple pieces.

Makes about 20 slices.

BASIL-CHEESE TOASTS

2 tomatoes
45 g (1½ oz) canned flat anchovy fillets, well drained
10 slices French bread
125 g (4 oz) Gruyére cheese
pepper
4 tablespoons finely shredded basil leaves
4 tablespoons olive oil
10 calamatta olives, if desired
fresh basil leaves, to garnish

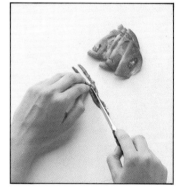

Slice the tomatoes thinly; if the tomatoes are large, halve the slices. Cut the anchovies into long strips.

Place the bread in a shallow oiled ovenproof dish. Grate the cheese and divide among the slices of French bread. Arrange the anchovy strips on top, then add a tomato slice or two. Grind some pepper over and sprinkle with some of the fresh basil.

Drizzle the olive oil over and cook at 200C (400F/Gas 6) for 10 to 15 minutes, until the bread is crisp and the cheese has melted. Sprinkle the remaining basil over and place a calamatta olive on top of each, if desired. Serve hot.

Makes 10.

EGG & CHIVE PINWHEELS

1 loaf unsliced white bread
125 g (4 oz) butter, at room temperature
6 hard-boiled eggs
3 tablespoons mayonnaise
1 teaspoon hot English mustard
salt and pepper, to taste
6 tablespoons snipped fresh chives

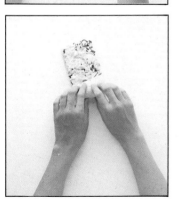

Using an electric or serrated edged knife, cut the bread lengthwise into 5 slices. Cut away the crusts. Spread each slice with the butter.

Shell the eggs and mash with the mayonnaise and mustard. Season to taste with salt and pepper. Spread evenly on the slices of bread, almost to the edges. Sprinkle the chives over.

Roll up each slice of bread. Chill in cling film (plastic wrap) until ready to serve. Using a serrated or electric knife, cut each roll into 5 or 6 slices. Arrange on a platter.

Makes 25 to 30.

EGG TAPENADE

6 hard-boiled eggs
18 black olives
5 canned anchovy fillets, drained
1 tablespoon drained capers
100 g (3½ oz) canned tuna, drained
3 tablespoons olive oil
lemon juice, to taste
fresh parsley leaves, to garnish

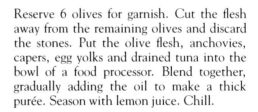

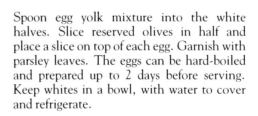

Shell the eggs and halve crosswise using a stainless steel knife. Remove the yolks and trim bases so eggs stand upright.

Reserve 6 olives for garnish. Cut the flesh away from the remaining olives and discard the stones. Put the olive flesh, anchovies, capers, egg yolks and drained tuna into the bowl of a food processor. Blend together, gradually adding the oil to make a thick purée. Season with lemon juice. Chill.

Spoon egg yolk mixture into the white halves. Slice reserved olives in half and place a slice on top of each egg. Garnish with parsley leaves. The eggs can be hard-boiled and prepared up to 2 days before serving. Keep whites in a bowl, with water to cover and refrigerate.

Makes 12.

DEVILLED EGGS

12 eggs
1 teaspoon prepared English mustard
6 tablespoons mayonnaise
few drops of Tabasco sauce
pinch of cayenne pepper
2 teaspoons paprika
rolled anchovy fillets, to garnish
salt

To boil eggs so the yolks are centred, tightly pack into a saucepan, pointed end down. Add water to cover, bring to the boil and cook for 10 minutes. Cook in 1 or 2 batches.

Drain the eggs and place under cold running water until they are cool. (Quick cooling prevents a black ring forming around the yolk.) Shell and halve the eggs using a stainless steel or silver knife (carbon steel will leave a black mark on the whites). Mash the yolks with the remaining ingredients, except anchovies, and season to taste with salt. Put into a piping bag.

If preparing ahead, store the yolk filling in the piping bag and the whites in a bowl of water to cover in the refrigerator. Drain the whites. Pipe the filling into the whites and decorate the top of each with an anchovy fillet.

Makes 24.

EGG & SESAME ROLLS

3 eggs
salt
1 tablespoon water
2 tablespoons sesame seeds
2 teaspoons soy sauce
¼ teaspoon sugar
½ small onion, finely chopped
250 g (8 oz) packet frozen spinach, defrosted and
    drained
1 thick slice cooked ham, cut into 3 strips

Lightly beat eggs with ¼ teaspoon salt and water. Make 3 thin omelettes. Stir sesame seeds in a dry pan over a low heat until golden, then grind while hot. Gently cook onion in a little oil, add drained spinach and season with salt to taste. Cool.

Place 1 omelette on a Japanese bamboo mat, rounded side up, and spread one-third of the spinach mixture on one end, taking care not to spread right up to the sides. Sprinkle with one-third of the sesame mixture and place a strip of ham down the centre.

Lift the mat so the omelette forms a roll, then roll again in the mat and press firmly. Leave for a few minutes, then unroll mat and cut the omelette roll into pieces. If liked, sprinkle with extra sesame seeds before serving.

Makes about 18.

AIOLI & CRUDITÉS

4 cloves garlic
½ teaspoon salt
2 egg yolks
250 ml (8 fl oz / 1 cup) virgin olive oil
juice of ½ lemon
crisp vegetables, such as carrots, celery and radish,
   to serve

Crush the garlic into a bowl, add the salt and egg yolks. Whisk together well. Add 1 or 2 drops of oil and whisk.

Continue whisking the egg yolk mixture, gradually adding the oil until about 2 table-spoons of the oil has been added. Add the remaining oil in a fine stream, whisking all the time. If the mixture becomes too thick, add a little hot water. Add the lemon juice and season with more salt, if needed. Cover and refrigerate.

Peel carrot and cut into 10 cm (4 in) lengths. Cut celery the same size and trim stem and root from radishes. Pile around the Aioli on a large platter. The vegetables are dipped into the Aioli before eating. Other vegetables such as mange tout (snow peas), cucumber sticks, fresh cauliflower florets, blanched asparagus tips and spring onions go well.

Serves 6 to 8.

EGG & CAVIAR SPREAD

4 eggs
60 g (2 oz) butter
salt and pepper
4 tablespoons thick sour cream
½ small onion, or 4 spring onions, finely chopped
3 tablespoons black caviar
biscuits (crackers), to serve
spring onion strips, to garnish

Put the eggs into a saucepan of cold water. Bring to the boil and cook for 10 minutes. Cool under running water and remove shells when cool enough to handle.

Mash the eggs finely using a potato masher. Melt the butter and pour, while hot, on to the warm eggs. Season with salt and pepper. Pack the egg mixture into a serving dish and chill. This can be prepared 1 day in advance.

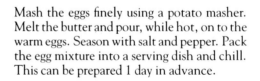

Combine the sour cream with the onion. Just before serving, spread sour cream mixture over the egg. Top with the black caviar and spring onion strips. Serve with biscuits (crackers).

Serves 6 to 8.

PISSALADIÈRE

3 sheets puff pastry or 1½/350 g (12 oz) packets
   frozen puff pastry, defrosted
3 or 4 tomatoes
pepper
6-8 calamatta olives
1 egg, beaten, to glaze
45 g (1½ oz) canned anchovy fillets

Cut each sheet of pastry into two 12 x 15 cm (5 x 6 in) rectangles. Place on greased baking tray. If using block pastry, roll out thinly and cut into rectangles. Cut the trimmings into 1½ cm (½ in) strips and place along edges of the pastry squares to form borders.

Prick the centre of the pastry with a fork. Halve the tomatoes and cut into slices. Arrange slices, overlapping, in rows on the pastry. Generously grind pepper over the top.

Cut the olive flesh away from the stones and place on the tomatoes. Drain the anchovies and arrange the strips on top. Brush the borders of the pastries with beaten egg and bake at 200C (400F/Gas 6) for 5 minutes, until golden. Serve warm, cutting each rectangle into quarters.

Makes 24 wedges.

MINI PIZZAS

15 g (½ oz) fresh (compressed) yeast
1 teaspoon sugar
250 ml (8 oz/1 cup) lukewarm water
300 g (10 oz/2½ cups) plain flour
½ teaspoon salt
2 onions, chopped
2 cloves garlic, crushed
2 tablespoons oil
4 to 6 tomatoes, skinned and sliced
2 teaspoons tomato paste
salt and pepper
125 g (4 oz) sliced spicy Italian salami
125 g (4 oz) mozzarella cheese
20 black olives

Cream the yeast with the sugar until it forms a liquid. Mix in the water.

Add yeast mixture to the flour and salt in a large bowl and form a dough. Knead for at least 5 minutes on a well floured surface. Turn into a greased bowl, cover and leave in a warm place about 1 hour, until double in bulk. Meanwhile, gently sauté the onion and garlic in oil for 2 minutes. Add the tomatoes and simmer until the sauce thickens, about 20 minutes. Stir in the tomato paste and season. Cut salami into quarters, the cheese into small pieces and the olives into chunks.

Turn the dough on to a board, knead lightly and roll out until 1 cm (½ in) thick. Cut into rounds with a 7.5 cm (3 in) cutter. Place on greased baking trays and top with sauce, then salami, cheese and olives. Bake at 200C (400F/Gas 6) for 20 to 30 minutes.

Makes about 12.

PEPPER PIZZETTES

PIZZA DOUGH:
450 g (1 lb/4 cups) strong plain flour
Pinch salt
15 g (½ oz) packet dried yeast
1 teaspoon granulated sugar
200 ml (7 fl oz/scant cup) warm water
2 tablespoons extra virgin olive oil
Fresh herb sprigs to garnish
TOPPING:
2 red or yellow peppers (capsicums)
3 tablespoons sun-dried tomato paste
4 tablespoons capers in wine vinegar, drained
2 tablespoons chopped fresh oregano
Salt and freshly ground black pepper

Preheat oven to 230C (450F/Gas 8). Oil two baking sheets. Turn dough onto a lightly floured surface. Knead gently then cut into 16 equal pieces. Roll each piece into a small oval about 5 mm (¼ inch) thick.

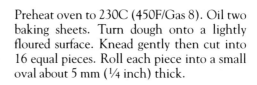

Sieve flour and salt into a large mixing bowl. In a small bowl, mix yeast, sugar and warm water. Leave for 10-15 minutes, until frothy. Stir oil into yeast then gradually beat into flour using a wooden spoon to give a soft, but not wet, dough. Turn onto a floured surface; knead for 5 minutes until smooth and elastic. Put into an oiled mixing bowl, cover and leave in a warm place for 35-40 minutes until doubled in size.

Transfer to the baking sheets and prick dough with a fork. Divide sun-dried tomato paste, reserved peppers (capsicums), capers and oregano between dough ovals. Season with salt and freshly ground black pepper. Bake in the preheated oven for 8-10 minutes, until golden. Serve hot or warm garnished with herb sprigs.

Makes 16 pizzettes.

Preheat grill. Cook whole peppers (capsicums) under the hot grill for about 10 minutes, turning occasionally, until evenly blistered and charred. Transfer to a plastic bag for a few minutes, then peel away and discard skins. De-seed peppers (capsicums) and cut into strips. Set aside.

Variations:
Red onion and Gorgonzola Replace above topping with 115 g (4 oz) crumbled Gorgonzola cheese; ½ red onion, chopped and 2 tablespoons chopped fresh thyme.

Prawn and fennel Instead of the peppers (capsicums), capers and herbs use 1 small fennel bulb, brushed with olive oil, roasted at 180C (350F/Gas 4) for 35-40 minutes, then cooled and chopped, 115 g (4 oz) peeled prawns and 2 teaspoons fennel seeds.

FOCACCIA

450 g (1 lb/4 cups) strong plain flour
Pinch salt
15 g (½ oz) packet dried yeast
225 ml (8 fl oz/1 cup) warm milk
1 teaspoon granulated sugar
4 tablespoons extra virgin olive oil, plus extra for
    brushing
2 teaspoons fresh rosemary leaves
Coarse sea salt

Sieve flour and salt into a large mixing bowl.
In a small bowl, mix together yeast, milk and
sugar. Leave for 10-15 minutes, until frothy.

Stir in oil then gradually beat into flour
mixture using wooden spoon to give a soft,
but not wet, dough; add a little more warm
milk if necessary. Turn dough onto a floured
surface; knead for 5 minutes until smooth and
elastic. Place in an oiled bowl, cover and
leave in a warm place for about 40 minutes
until doubled in size. Turn onto a floured
surface and knead for 5 minutes.

Preheat oven to 230C (450F/Gas 8). Oil a
baking sheet. Roll dough to a large circle
about 1.5 cm (½ inch) thick and transfer to
the baking sheet. Brush with olive oil and
sprinkle over rosemary and sea salt, pressing
in lightly. With a clean finger make deep
indentations over surface of dough. Leave to
rise for 25 minutes. Bake in the preheated
oven for 20-25 minutes until golden. Brush
again with olive oil. Serve warm.

Makes 1 loaf.

BREAD SALAD

225 g (8 oz) firm, country bread, crusts removed
1 red onion, thinly sliced
½ cucumber, peeled and diced
6 small tomatoes, quartered
2 sticks celery, sliced
6 sprigs fresh basil, shredded
9 stoned black olives, halved
Salt and freshly ground black pepper
5 tablespoons extra virgin olive oil
2 tablespoons red wine vinegar
1 teaspoon balsamic vinegar

Cut bread into small dice and place in a bowl.
Sprinkle with sufficient cold water to moisten
thoroughly but do not allow bread to become
soggy.

Add onion, cucumber tomatoes, celery, basil
and olives to bowl. Season with salt and
freshly ground black pepper. In a small bowl,
mix together oil and vinegars then pour over
salad. Toss well to mix. Leave to stand for 30
minutes before serving.

Serves 6.

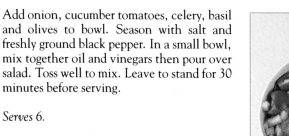

TOMATO & ONION BREAD

450 g (1 lb/4 cups) strong plain flour
Pinch salt
15 g (½ oz) packet dried yeast
1 teaspoon granulated sugar
200 ml (7 fl oz/scant cup) warm water
4 tablespoons extra virgin olive oil
1 onion, finely chopped
1 clove garlic, crushed
115 g (4 oz) sun-dried tomatoes preserved in oil,
    drained
9 large fresh basil leaves
Freshly ground black pepper
Milk to glaze
1 teaspoon coarse sea salt

Oil a baking sheet. Heat remaining oil in a frying pan, add onion and garlic and cook for 3 minutes, to soften. Remove from the heat and set aside. Turn dough onto a lightly floured surface and cut in half. Roll out to give two identical rectangles about 23 × 30 cm (9 × 12 inches). Transfer one piece to the baking sheet and prick surface with a fork.

Sieve flour and salt into a large mixing bowl. In a small bowl mix yeast, sugar and warm water. Leave for 10-15 minutes until frothy.

Spread reserved onion mixture over pricked dough, leaving a 1.5 cm (½ inch) border around edge. Top with sun-dried tomatoes and basil leaves and season with freshly ground black pepper. Moisten edges of dough with a little cold water and cover with second rectangle of dough.

Oil a mixing bowl. Stir 3 tablespoons of the olive oil into yeast mixture then, using a wooden spoon, gradually mix into flour to give a soft, but not wet, dough. Turn onto a lightly floured surface and knead for 5 minutes until smooth and elastic. Put into the oiled bowl, cover and leave in a warm place for 35-40 minutes until doubled in size.

Preheat oven to 230C (450F/Gas 8). Crimp edges of the dough to seal and using a sharp knife mark a lattice pattern on the surface. Brush the dough with a little milk to glaze and sprinkle with the coarse sea salt. Leave to rise for 25 minutes. Bake in the preheated oven for about 25 minutes until golden brown and the underside is firm and lightly coloured. Serve warm or cold, on its own as part of the antipasti.

Makes 1 large loaf.

GOATS CHEESE TARTS

1-2 teaspoons extra virgin olive oil
25 g (1 oz) butter
115 g (4 oz/2 cups) soft white breadcrumbs
1 tablespoon sesame seeds
175 g (6 oz/¾ cup) soft goats cheese
4 sun-dried tomatoes in oil, drained
4 basil fresh leaves
1 teaspoon finely chopped fresh mint
Salt and freshly ground black pepper
Mixed salad leaves to garnish, if desired

Use olive oil to grease four 7.5-10 cm (3-4 inch) tartlet tins.

Preheat oven to 200C (400F/Gas 6). Melt butter in a small saucepan and stir in breadcrumbs and sesame seeds. Divide between prepared tartlet tins, pressing firmly into base and sides. Bake in the preheated oven for 12-15 minutes until crisp and light golden. Carefully remove tartlets from tins and place on a baking sheet.

Divide goats cheese between tartlets and top each with a sun-dried tomato. Season with salt and freshly ground black pepper. Return to oven for 8-10 minutes to heat through. Serve hot or warm with a basil leaf and a sprinkling of chopped mint on each tart. Garnish with mixed salad leaves, if desired.

Serves 4.

BRUSCHETTA AL POMODORO

8 small thick slices country bread
55 ml (2 fl oz/¼ cup) extra virgin olive oil
1 clove garlic, crushed
2 ripe beefsteak tomatoes, chopped
2 tablespoons chopped fresh basil
8 canned anchovy fillets, drained, if desired
Salt and freshly ground black pepper

Preheat oven to 200C (400F/Gas 6). Put bread in one layer on a baking sheet and bake in the preheated oven for 10 minutes until golden.

Meanwhile warm oil and garlic in a small saucepan.

Trickle oil and garlic over bread. Divide tomatoes and basil between slices, season with salt and freshly ground black pepper and top with anchovy fillets, if desired. Serve at once.

Serves 4.

OLIVE BREAD

700 g (1½ lbs/6 cups) strong plain flour
Pinch salt
1 tablespoon chopped fresh oregano
15 g (½ oz) packet dried yeast
1 teaspoon granulated sugar
325 ml (11 fl oz/1⅓ cups) warm water
4 tablespoons extra virgin olive oil, plus extra for
    brushing
30 stoned green olives

Sieve flour and salt into a large bowl; stir in oregano. In a small bowl mix together yeast, sugar and warm water. Leave 10-15 minutes until frothy.

Stir oil into yeast liquid then gradually add to flour mixture beating well with a wooden spoon, to give a soft, but not wet, dough; add a little more warm water if necessary.

Oil a bowl. Turn dough onto a lightly floured surface and knead for 5 minutes until elastic. Place dough in the bowl, cover and leave in a warm place for about 40 minutes until doubled in size.

Oil 1 or 2 baking sheets. Turn dough onto a floured surface. To make one large loaf roll out to a large circle, 2.5 cm (1 inch) thick. Or cut the dough in half and roll out two ovals just over 1.5 cm (½ inch) thick. Place on the baking sheet or sheets.

With a clean floured finger make 30 deep indentations over surface of large loaf, or 15 for each small one. Press an olive into each indentation.

Preheat oven to 230C (450F/Gas 8). Brush loaves with olive oil and leave to rise for 25 minutes. Bake in the preheated oven for 20-25 minutes for small loaves, 30-35 minutes for a large loaf until a rich golden brown and underside sounds hollow when tapped. Cool on a wire rack. Serve warm or cold as part of the antipasti.

Makes 1 large or 2 small loaves.

CRAB & RICOTTA TARTS

PASTRY:
225 g (8 oz/2 cups) plain (all-purpose) flour
Pinch salt
115 g (4 oz) butter, diced
FILLING:
225 g (8 oz) crab meat
225 g (8 oz/1 cup) ricotta cheese
3 spring onions (scallions), finely chopped
2 whole eggs plus 1 yolk
2 tablespoons chopped fresh Italian parsley
Few drops Tabasco (hot pepper sauce)
Salt and freshly ground black pepper
Mixed salad leaves to serve
Fresh Italian parsley sprigs to garnish

Preheat oven to 200C (400F/Gas 6). Sieve flour and salt into a mixing bowl; rub in butter until mixture resembles breadcrumbs. Stir in about 4 tablespoons cold water to make to a firm dough. Turn onto a floured surface; knead gently until smooth. Use to line four 10 cm (4 inch) tartlet tins. Prick bases with a fork; chill for 20 minutes. Line pastry cases with greaseproof paper and fill with baking beans. Bake in the preheated oven for 15 minutes, removing beans and paper after 10 minutes.

Remove tartlet cases from oven and turn temperature to 180C (350F/Gas 4). Mix filling ingredients together in a bowl. Spoon into tartlet cases. Bake in the oven for about 20 minutes until set and golden brown. Serve warm or cold with a few mixed salad leaves and garnish with Italian parsley sprigs.

Serves 4.

SAVOURY PASTIES

1 quantity Pizza Dough recipe, see page 74
Vegetable oil for deep frying
Fresh Italian parsley sprigs to garnish
FILLING:
3 tablespoons sun-dried tomato paste
2 tablespoons olive paste
175 g (6 oz) mozzarella cheese, thinly sliced
Salt and freshly ground black pepper
1 egg white, lightly beaten

Make pizza dough and put to rise for 30 minutes until doubled in size.

Turn dough onto a lightly floured surface and roll out to 5 mm (¼ inch) thickness. Stamp out circles using a 10 cm (4 inch) plain round biscuit cutter. Spread a little sun-dried tomato paste and olive paste onto each round of dough. Cut mozzarella slices in half and put a piece on each dough circle. Season with salt and ground black pepper.

Brush edges of dough with a little egg white then fold dough over filling to make half-moon shapes, pressing edges to seal. Half-fill a deep-fat frying pan with oil. Preheat to 180C (350F). Deep fry a few pasties at a time, in the hot oil for 2-3 minutes, turning once, until golden. Using a slotted spoon, transfer to absorbent kitchen paper to drain. Serve hot garnished with Italian parsley sprigs.

Makes about 12.

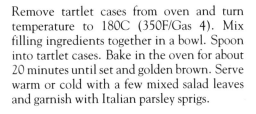

WALNUT BREAD

15 g (½ oz) sachet dried yeast
150 ml (5 fl oz/⅔ cup) warm milk
1 tablespoon clear honey
350 g (12 oz/3 cups) strong plain flour
350 g (12 oz/3 cups) plain wholemeal flour
1½ teaspoons salt
25 g (1 oz) butter, diced
150 g (5 oz/1¼ cups) walnuts, chopped
2 teaspoons fennel seeds, lightly crushed
½ teaspoon grated nutmeg
Milk to glaze

In a small bowl or jug mix yeast with warm milk and honey. Leave for 10-15 minutes until frothy.

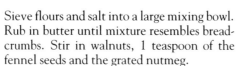

Sieve flours and salt into a large mixing bowl. Rub in butter until mixture resembles breadcrumbs. Stir in walnuts, 1 teaspoon of the fennel seeds and the grated nutmeg.

Using a wooden spoon, stir yeast liquid into flour mixture with sufficient warm water to form a soft, but not wet, dough.

Oil a mixing bowl. Turn dough out onto a lightly floured surface and knead for 5 minutes until elastic. Put into an oiled mixing bowl, cover and leave in a warm place for 35-40 minutes until doubled in size. Turn onto a lightly floured surface and knead again for 5 minutes.

Preheat oven to 220C (425F/Gas 7). Oil a deep 15 cm (6 inch) round cake tin. Divide dough into seven equal sized pieces and shape into balls. Arrange in the cake tin. Brush tops with milk and sprinkle with remaining 1 teaspoon fennel seeds. Leave in a warm place for 25 minutes then bake in the oven for about 45 minutes until the top is well browned and the bottom sounds hollow when tapped.

Turn bread onto a wire rack and leave to cool. Serve as part of the antipasti.

Makes 1 large loaf.

Note: This bread is delicious served with cheese and fish dishes, for soaking up olive oil dressings and is particularly good toasted.

MOZZARELLA TOASTS

12 thick slices French stick or slim Italian loaf
70 ml (2½ fl oz/⅓ cup) extra virgin olive oil
1 teaspoon finely chopped fresh Italian parsley
14 anchovy fillets canned in oil, drained
450 g (1 lb) mozzarella cheese, cut into 12 slices
Freshly ground black pepper
Fresh Italian parsley sprigs to garnish

Preheat grill. Arrange bread in one layer on a baking sheet. Toast both sides until golden.

Meanwhile put oil, parsley and two of the anchovy fillets in a small saucepan. Heat gently to warm, stirring with a fork to break up anchovies. Trickle oil mixture over toasted bread and top each piece with a slice of mozzarella. Season with freshly ground black pepper.

Garnish toasts with remaining anchovy fillets and return to grill for 2-3 minutes until cheese is hot and bubbling. Serve at once garnished with Italian parsley sprigs.

Serves 6.

OLIVE PASTE TOASTS

4 large thick slices country bread
3 tablespoons extra virgin olive oil
½ clove garlic, crushed
Red pepper (capsicum) strips and fresh thyme sprigs to garnish
OLIVE PASTE:
175 g (6 oz/1¼ cups) stoned black olives
2 tablespoons extra virgin olive oil
Few drops balsamic vinegar
Salt and freshly ground black pepper

Preheat oven to 200C (400F/Gas 6). To make olive paste put ingredients in a food processor or blender and process until fairly smooth. Transfer to a bowl and set aside.

Cut each slice of bread into 3 fingers. Place on a baking sheet and bake in the preheated oven for 10-12 minutes until golden and crisp. Meanwhile, warm oil with garlic in a small saucepan.

Trickle oil and garlic over bread. Serve at once spread with olive paste and garnished with red pepper (capsicum) strips and thyme sprigs.

Serves 4-6.

Note: Olive paste can be made in advance or in larger quantities. Put into jars, pour over olive oil to cover and seal and keep in refrigerator for up to 1 month.

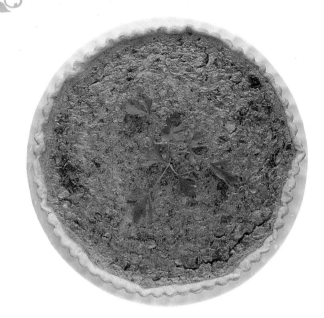

MUSHROOM TART

PASTRY:
225 g (8 oz/2 cups) plain (all-purpose) flour
Pinch salt
115 g (4 oz) butter, diced
Fresh Italian parsley sprigs to garnish
FILLING:
25 g (1 oz) dried ceps (porcini)
25 g (1 oz) butter, diced
1 medium onion, finely chopped
115 g (4 oz) button mushrooms, chopped
2 tablespoons finely chopped fresh Italian parsley
1 tablespoon sun-dried tomato paste
4 tablespoons single (light) cream
3 large eggs
25 g (1 oz/¼ cup) freshly grated Parmesan cheese
Salt and freshly ground black pepper

Melt butter in a medium saucepan. Add onion and button mushrooms and cook gently for 5 minutes to soften. Stir in ceps (porcini), parsley and sun-dried tomato paste. Cook for a further 2 minutes then stir in cream. Continue to cook over a low heat for 8-10 minutes until liquid is reduced by half. Remove from heat and allow to cool.

To make pastry, sieve flour and salt into a mixing bowl, add butter and rub in until mixture resembles breadcrumbs. Stir in 4-5 tablespoons cold water to make to a firm dough. Wrap in plastic wrap and put in refrigerator while preparing filling.

Roll out dough and use to line the flan ring. Prick base with a fork. Line pastry case with greaseproof paper and cover with baking beans. Bake 'blind' in the preheated oven for 25 minutes, removing beans and paper for last 5 minutes. Turn oven temperature to 190C (375F/Gas 5).

Preheat oven to 200C (400F/Gas 6). Grease a 23 cm (9 inch) flan ring. Put dried ceps (porcini) in a small bowl. Cover generously with warm water and leave to soak for 20 minutes. Drain and rinse to remove any grit. Dry briefly on absorbent kitchen paper then chop finely and set aside.

Beat eggs in a large jug or bowl. Stir in Parmesan and cooled mushroom mixture. Season with salt and freshly ground black pepper then pour into pastry case. Bake for about 20 minutes until set. Serve warm or cold garnished with parsley sprigs.

Serves 8.

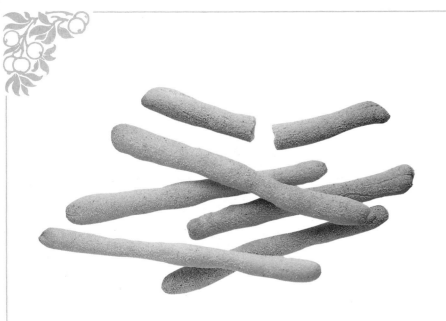

GRISSINI

450 g (1 lb) strong plain flour
½ teaspoon salt
25 g (1 oz) grated Parmesan or provolone cheese
7 g (¼ oz) dry yeast
1 teaspoon granulated sugar
300 ml (10 fl oz/1¼ cups) warm water
2 tablespoons extra virgin olive oil plus extra for oiling
85 g (3 oz/1 cup) polenta (corn meal)

Sieve flour and salt into a large mixing bowl. Stir in cheese. In a small bowl mix yeast, sugar and warm water. Leave for 10-15 minutes until frothy.

Stir olive oil into frothy yeast liquid then beat into flour using a wooden spoon to give a soft dough. Turn onto a floured surface and knead for 5 minutes until smooth and elastic. Lightly oil a baking sheet. Roll out dough to a large rectangle and transfer to prepared baking sheet. Brush the surface with a little oil, cover loosely and leave in a warm place for 35-40 minutes until doubled in size.

Preheat oven to 230C (450F/Gas 8). Oil 2 more baking sheets. Cut dough into 24 equal pieces. Sprinkle polenta on work surface. Using your hands, roll each piece of dough to a thin stick about 23 cm (9 inches) long.

Arrange slightly apart on the baking sheets and bake in the preheated oven for 15-20 minutes until golden and crisp. Cool on wire racks. Serve warm or cold as part of the antipasti.

Makes 24.

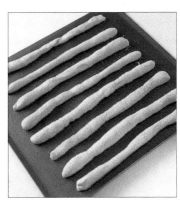

Variation: Replace polenta with 85 g (3 oz) sesame seeds.

DEVILLED CRAB QUICHE

250 g (8 oz/2 cups) plain flour
½ teaspoon salt
½ teaspoon chilli seasoning
60 g (2 oz/¼ cup) block margarine, diced
60 g (2 oz/¼ cup) lard, diced
60 g (2 oz/½ cup) finely grated Cheddar cheese
6 rashers streaky bacon, chopped
1 onion, chopped
125 g (4 oz) crabmeat, flaked
3 eggs
155 ml (5 fl oz/⅔ cup) single (light) cream
½ teaspoon dry mustard
¼ teaspoon cayenne pepper
tomato and sprig of parsley, to garnish

Preheat oven to 200C (400F/Gas 6).

Put flour, salt and chilli seasoning into a bowl. Add margarine and lard and rub in finely until mixture resembles breadcrumbs. Add cheese and mix well. Stir in 3 tablespoons water and mix to form a firm dough. Knead gently. Roll out pastry and use to line a 25 cm (10 in) loose-bottomed, fluted flan tin, set on a baking sheet. Press pastry well into flutes and trim edge neatly. Prick base all over with a fork. Line flan with a piece of greaseproof paper and fill with baking beans.

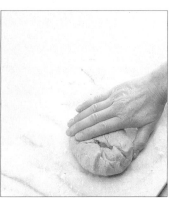

Bake in the oven for 15 minutes, then remove paper and beans and return flan to oven for a further 5-10 minutes until dry and lightly golden. Meanwhile, dry-fry bacon in a pan for 3 minutes. Add onion and cook for 2 minutes. Remove from heat and mix with crabmeat. Spoon mixture into flan case. Whisk together eggs, cream, mustard and cayenne and season with salt. Pour into flan case. Bake for 30-35 minutes until golden. Serve, garnished with tomato and parsley.

Serves 6-8.

CHILLI PEPPER PIZZA

3 tablespoons olive oil
1 onion, quartered and sliced
1 clove garlic, crushed
250 g (8 oz) can tomatoes
1 tablespoon tomato purée (paste)
½ teaspoon dried oregano
125 g (4 oz/1 cup) plain flour
125 g (4 oz/1 cup) plain wholewheat flour
¼ teaspoon salt
1 teaspoon easy blend dried yeast
155 ml (5 fl oz/⅔ cup) hand-hot water
100 g (3½ oz) can green chillies in brine
185 g (6 oz) Mozzarella cheese, chopped
60 g (2 oz) pepperoni salami sticks, sliced
8 black or green olives
tomato roses and sprigs of parsley, to garnish

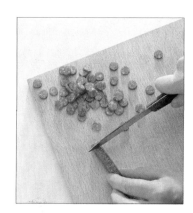

Heat 2 tablespoons oil in a saucepan. Add onion, garlic, tomatoes, tomato purée (paste) and oregano. Stir well to break up tomatoes, then simmer, uncovered, for 10-15 minutes until well thickened. Leave to cool. Preheat oven to 190C (375F/Gas 5). Put flours, salt and yeast into a bowl and mix well. Add water and mix to form a dough. Knead well, then roll out to a round large enough to line a lightly greased 25 cm (10 in) pizza tray.

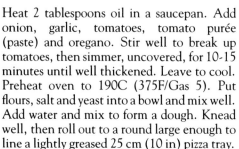

Brush surface of dough with a little of the remaining oil and cover with tomato mixture. Drain and chop chillies and sprinkle on top. Scatter with chopped cheese and drizzle with remaining oil. Bake in the oven for 25 minutes. Add sliced pepperoni and olives to pizza and continue cooking for a further 10 minutes. Serve hot, cut into wedges, garnished with tomato roses and sprigs of parsley.

Serves 2 (as a meal) or 4 (as a snack).

LAMB TRIANGLES

1 clove garlic, crushed
1 teaspoon grated fresh root ginger
1 onion, finely chopped
1 tablespoon oil
1 tablespoon curry powder
1 tablespoon white distilled vinegar
250 g (8 oz) lean minced cooked lamb
125 ml (4 fl oz / ½ cup) water
2 tablespoons chopped mint
salt
1 egg, beaten
3 sheets filo pastry
melted butter, to glaze

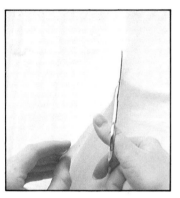

Cook garlic, ginger and onion in oil for 1 minute. Add curry powder and stir for another minute. Add vinegar, lamb and water and simmer for 5 minutes. Add mint and season to taste. Mix in egg, then cool. Cut pastry into 5 cm (2 in) wide strips. Keep pastry covered with a damp cloth to prevent drying out.

Layer two strips of pastry and brush with melted butter. Put a spoonful of filling in 1 corner and fold the pastry over the filling.

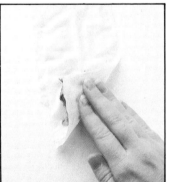

Continue to fold pastry over, keeping the triangular shape. Brush top with melted butter and place on buttered baking trays. Repeat until all are made. Bake at 200C (400F/Gas 6) for 20 minutes or until golden and crisp. Cool slightly before serving.

Makes 24.

MUSHROOM PASTIES

125 g (4 oz / 1 cup) plain flour
90 g (3 oz) butter
1 tablespoon water
3 spring onions, chopped
250 g (8 oz) button mushrooms, chopped
1 tablespoon plain flour
1 tablespoon dry sherry
¼ teaspoon dry mustard
2 tablespoons milk
8 olives, sliced
salt and pepper
1 egg beaten, to glaze

Sift flour into a bowl and rub in 60 g (2 oz) butter. Add the water to make a firm dough. Wrap and chill.

Sauté the onions in the remaining butter in a frying pan, without browning. Add the mushrooms and cook, stirring, until all the liquid evaporates. Stir in the flour and mix well. Add the sherry, mustard and milk and stir until mixture boils. Add the olives and season to taste. Allow this mushroom filling to cool.

Thinly roll out the pastry on a floured surface and cut into 7.5 cm (3 in) rounds. Brush edges with egg. Put a good teaspoonful of the filling in the centre of each round. Bring up the edges to join and pinch together. Place on greased baking trays, brush with egg to glaze and bake at 200C (400F/Gas 6) for 25 to 20 minutes.

Makes 10.

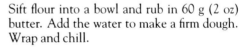

RICOTTA CHEESE BALLS

SPINACH & FETA ROLLS

1 kg (2 lb) Ricotta cheese
1 red pepper (capsicum), finely chopped
4 tablespoons finely chopped mixed fresh herbs
4 tablespoons black or toasted sesame seeds
1 teaspoon salt

Keep the Ricotta cheese well chilled. Form into 24 balls with a small ice cream scoop or a spoon. Divide the Ricotta balls into three groups. Roll the first group in the finely chopped red pepper. Place on a foil-lined tray and chill.

2 tablespoons vegetable oil
2 onions, finely chopped
250 g (8 oz) packet frozen spinach, defrosted and drained
2 teaspoons dried dill
125 g (4 oz) feta cheese, crumbled
1 egg, beaten
3 tablespoons thick sour cream
12 sheets filo pastry
125 g (4 oz) butter, melted

Gently heat oil in a saucepan and sauté the onions until tender, but not coloured. Add the spinach and sauté for a further 2 minutes. Add the dill and feta cheese.

Roll the next group of balls in the chopped herbs. Some chopped spring onion may be added for more flavour.

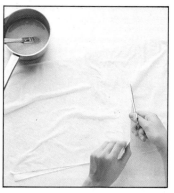

Remove from the heat and allow to cool. Mix in the egg and sour cream. Chill. Take 1 sheet of the filo pastry, (keep remaining sheets covered with damp absorbent paper) and brush with butter. Top with another sheet of filo and cut into 3 strips.

Mix the black sesame seeds (available from Asian food shops) with the salt and roll the last balls in this. Chill all the Ricotta balls. To serve, arrange rows of the colourful balls on a platter.

Makes 24.

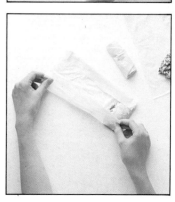

Spoon 1 tablespoon of the spinach mixture on one end of a strip and roll up, tucking in the edges. Brush the end with more butter to seal. Repeat with the remaining pastry and spinach filling. Place the rolls joined end down on baking trays and bake at 200C (400F/Gas 6) for about 15 minutes. Serve hot.

Makes 18.

CURRY PIES

1 onion, chopped
1 tablespoon vegetable oil
1 tablespoon curry powder
2 tablespoons vinegar
6 tablespoons water
500 g (1 lb) lean minced beef
1 teaspoon salt
2 tablespoons sultanas
2 teaspoons cornflour
250 g (8 oz) shortcrust pastry
water or 1 egg, beaten, to glaze

Sauté the onion in the oil for 2 minutes, stirring, until soft.

Add the curry powder and stir for 1 more minute. Add the vinegar, 4 tablespoons water and mix well. Stir in the meat, salt and sultanas, then cook for 10 minutes. Blend the cornflour with the remaining 2 tablespoons water and stir into the mixture. Cook for a further 2 minutes. Cool, then chill.

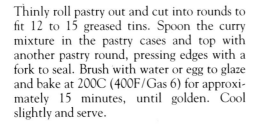

Thinly roll pastry out and cut into rounds to fit 12 to 15 greased tins. Spoon the curry mixture in the pastry cases and top with another pastry round, pressing edges with a fork to seal. Brush with water or egg to glaze and bake at 200C (400F/Gas 6) for approximately 15 minutes, until golden. Cool slightly and serve.

Makes 12 to 15.

HOT CHEESE & HAM PUFFS

60 g (2 oz / ½ cup) plain flour
125 ml (4 fl oz / ½ cup) water
90 g (3 oz) butter, diced
½ teaspoon salt
2 eggs
1 tablespoon extra plain flour
125 g (4 fl oz / ½ cup) milk
3 tablespoons finely grated Cheddar cheese
60 g (2 oz) lean cooked ham, finely chopped
3 tablespoons grated fresh Parmesan cheese

Sift flour on to a sheet of greaseproof paper. Heat water and 60 g (2 oz) of the butter with salt until butter melts.

Bring mixture to a full boil and add flour all at once. Stir until mixture forms a ball and leaves the side of the pan. Cool. Beat in the eggs, one at a time. Drop heaped teaspoonfuls of mixture on to greased baking trays. Bake at 200C (400F/Gas 6) for 25 to 30 minutes, until puffed and golden. Cool, cut halves and scoop out any soft centres.

Melt remaining butter in a small saucepan, stir in 1 tablespoon flour and cook for 1 minute. Add the milk and stir until sauce boils and thickens. Add the Cheddar cheese, then the ham. Season with salt and pepper. Spoon mixture into the puffs, replace tops and sprinkle with the Parmesan cheese. Return to the oven for 5 minutes to warm.

Makes about 20.

—SMOKED SALMON QUICHES—

½ x 375 g (12 oz) packet frozen puff pastry, defrosted
6 eggs
375 ml (12 fl oz / 1½ cups) heavy (thickened) cream
½ teaspoon salt
pinch of grated nutmeg
125 g (4 oz) finely chopped smoked salmon
black caviar, extra salmon and dill sprigs, to garnish

Roll out the pastry thinly. Cut into 24 rounds with a 6.5 cm (2½ in) cutter. Line greased patty tins with the pastry rounds.

Beat the eggs with the cream, salt and nutmeg until well mixed. Stir in the salmon. Spoon the mixture into the pastry cases, ensuring the salmon is evenly distributed.

Bake at 200C (400F/Gas 6) for 10 to 15 minutes or until puffed and golden. Serve warm. For large parties, the quiches may be cooked in advance, removed from the tins and chilled. To re-heat, place on flat trays and warm at 200C (400F/Gas 6) for 5 minutes.

Makes 24.

—ARTICHOKES WITH CAVIAR—

440 g (14 oz) can artichoke bottoms
3-6 slices white bread
2 tablespoons vegetable oil
2 tablespoons thick sour cream
1 tablespoon aioli or homemade mayonnaise
juice of ½ lemon
1 tablespoon snipped fresh chives
6 teaspoons black or red caviar

Drain the artichoke bottoms discarding the liquid in the can.

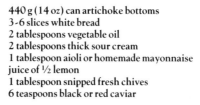

Cut out 6 rounds of bread using a biscuit cutter. Heat the oil in a shallow pan. When hot, fry the bread rounds until golden on both sides. Drain on absorbent paper. Combine the sour cream and aioli or mayonnaise, adding a few drops of lemon juice to taste, then stir in the snipped chives.

The bread can be prepared 24 hours in advance and stored in an airtight container, and the cream can be mixed and chilled ready to assemble at the last moment. Place the artichoke bottoms on the bread rounds, top with a spoonful of the sour cream mixture and the caviar.

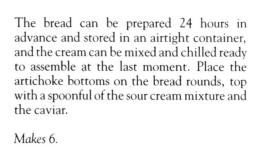

Makes 6.

QUICK DIPS

ORIENTAL PRAWNS

CREAMY CORN DIP

300 g (10 oz) jar, corn relish
300 ml (10 fl oz) carton thick sour cream
biscuits (crackers) or corn chips, to serve

Mix the jar of corn relish with the sour cream. Pile into a serving bowl and surround with biscuits or corn chips.

Serves 6 to 8.

CAVIAR DIP

300 ml (10 fl oz) carton thick sour cream
50 g (3 oz) jar red caviar
1 tablespoon finely chopped onion
fresh parsley sprig, to garnish
vegetable and biscuits (crackers), to serve

Mix the sour cream with half the caviar and the onion. Turn into a serving bowl and swirl in the rest of the caviar. Garnish with a parsley sprig and serve with vegetables or biscuits for dipping.

Serves 6 to 8.

ANCHOVY DIP

300 ml (10 fl oz) carton thick sour cream
25 g (1½ oz) can anchovy fillets, drained and mashed
3 tablespoons chopped dill pickles
2 teaspoons drained capers
biscuits (crackers), to serve

Blend sour cream, anchovies and pickles. Turn into a bowl and garnish with the capers. Serve with biscuits.

Serves 6 to 8.

8 raw Mediterranean (king) prawns
60 g (2 oz/½ cup) plain flour
¼ teaspoon salt
1 teaspoon corn oil
2.5 cm (1 inch) fresh root ginger, peeled and grated
1 clove garlic, crushed
1 teaspoon chilli sauce
1 egg white
vegetable oil for frying
spring onion tassel and few strips of red pepper, to garnish

Peel prawns, leaving tail shells on. Make a small incision along the spines. Remove black spinal cords from prawns.

Put flour into a bowl. Add salt, oil and 60 ml (2 fl oz/¼ cup) water and mix together. Stir in ginger, garlic and chilli sauce and beat well. In a bowl, whisk egg white until stiff, then gently fold into batter until evenly combined.

Half-fill a deep fat pan or fryer with oil and heat to 190C (375F) or until a cube of day-old bread browns in 40 seconds. Hold each prawn by its tail and dip it into batter, then lower it into hot oil. Fry for 3 minutes until golden. Drain on absorbent kitchen paper. Serve hot, garnished with spring onion tassel and red pepper strips.

Serves 4.

PEANUT SAUCE & CRUDITÉS

MEXICAN BEAN DIP

2 cloves garlic
2 tablespoons dark soy sauce
4 tablespoons smooth peanut butter
1 tablespoon sugar
250 ml (8 fl oz / 1 cup) water
2 red chillies
selection of crisp vegetables, such as carrots, celery, a
    cucumber, radishes and a cauliflower

Crush the garlic and place in a small saucepan with the soy sauce, peanut butter, sugar and water.

465 g (15 oz) canned red kidney beans
2 tablespoons vegetable oil
90 g (3 oz / ¾ cup) grated Cheddar cheese
½ teaspoon salt
1 teaspoon chilli powder
1 tablespoon chopped green pepper (capsicum)
corn chips or prawn crisps for dipping

Drain the beans, reserving the liquid for the dip.

Shred the chillies, removing the seeds. Put the chilli shreds into the pan and heat together. Simmer for 5 minutes stirring constantly. If the mixture is very thin, simmer until it thickens slightly. Leave to cool. The sauce sometimes becomes solid when cool. When this happens thin with a little water. Pour into a serving bowl.

Heat the oil in a small pan and add the beans, mashing with a potato masher as they cook. Add 3 tablespoons of the reserved bean liquid and stir in until well mixed. Cool. Add cheese, salt and chilli powder. If the mixture is thick, add more of the reserved bean liquid until it is a good consistency for scooping. Add the pepper. Serve hot with corn chips or prawn crisps.

Serves 4 to 6.

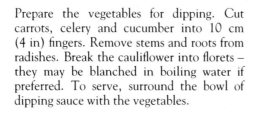

Prepare the vegetables for dipping. Cut carrots, celery and cucumber into 10 cm (4 in) fingers. Remove stems and roots from radishes. Break the cauliflower into florets – they may be blanched in boiling water if preferred. To serve, surround the bowl of dipping sauce with the vegetables.

Serves 4 to 6.

If using prawn crisps, drop a few at a time into deep hot oil. When they come to the top, remove almost immediately and drain. The crisps take only a few seconds to cook. Drain on absorbent paper and store in an airtight container until ready to use.

HUMMUS BI TAHINI

125 g (4 oz) chick-peas
salt
4 cloves garlic, crushed
125 g (4 oz / ½ cup) tahini paste
juice of 2 lemons
1 tablespoon olive oil
paprika and fresh parsley sprig, to garnish
pitta bread, to serve

Wash the chick-peas and soak overnight in water to cover.

Drain chick-peas. Add fresh water to cover and 2 teaspoons salt. Cover and simmer for 2 hours or until tender. Purée the chick-peas in a food processor, adding a little of the cooking liquid to make a smooth paste. Add the crushed garlic, tahini paste and lemon juice to taste.

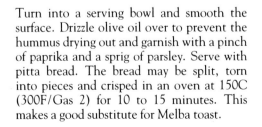

Turn into a serving bowl and smooth the surface. Drizzle olive oil over to prevent the hummus drying out and garnish with a pinch of paprika and a sprig of parsley. Serve with pitta bread. The bread may be split, torn into pieces and crisped in an oven at 150C (300F/Gas 2) for 10 to 15 minutes. This makes a good substitute for Melba toast.

Serves 12 to 15.

EGG & NORI ROLLS

3 eggs
salt
1 tablespoon cold water
2 sheets nori (sheets dried laver seaweed available from Asian food shops)

Beat the eggs with salt to taste and water until mixed. Set aside. Toast the sheets of nori by holding briefly over a gas flame. The nori may be also toasted by quickly running it across an electric hotplate set at a moderate heat. Take care not to burn the nori.

Reserve 1 teaspoonful of the egg mixture. Make 4 thin omelettes with the remaining egg mixture in a greased frying pan, cooking on one side only.

Place one omelette, uncooked side up, on a bamboo mat, top with the nori, trimmed to size, then another omelette until all are used. Roll up the omelettes in the mat and seal the edge with the reserved egg. Make a tight, compact roll and leave until cold. Remove the mat and cut into rolls.

Makes 6 to 8.

SKEWERED BITES

MINTED SAMBAL DIP

PARMA HAM (PROSCIUTTO) AND MELON

1 small cantaloupe (rock) melon
250 g (8 oz) very thinly sliced Parma ham (prosciutto)

Peel the melon, cut into halves and scoop out the seeds. Cut the flesh into cubes. Take a ham slice, gather up and skewer on to a melon cube with a wooden toothpick. Serve chilled.

Makes about 48.

AVOCADO AND PRAWN

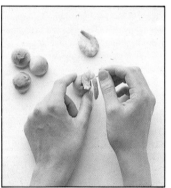

1 ripe avocado pear
500 g (1 lb) cooked prawns
juice of 1 lemon

Halve the avocado and remove the stone. Either scoop out the flesh with a melon baller or cut into cubes. Peel the prawns and de-vein. Skewer a prawn and piece of avocado together. Squeeze lemon juice over. Serve immediately.

Makes about 18.

SMOKED BEEF ROLLS

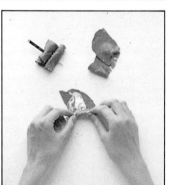

2 tablespoons sour cream
1 teaspoon horseradish sauce
125 g (4 oz) thinly sliced smoked beef

Mix together sour cream and horseradish, spread on beef and roll up. Cut into 2.5 cm (1 in) pieces and serve 2 or 3 rolls on a toothpick.

Makes 8 to 10.

4 spring onions
300 ml (10 fl oz) carton thick sour cream
1 teaspoon finely grated fresh root ginger
1 tablespoon lemon juice
1 tablespoon curry powder
6-8 tablespoons chopped fresh mint
1 clove garlic
1 teaspoon salt
fresh vegetables for dipping

Finely chop the spring onions including most of the green tops. Add to the sour cream with the ginger, lemon juice, curry powder and chopped mint. Mix well

Peel garlic and crush the clove in salt until it forms a pulp. Add to the sour cream mixture and stir in well. If mixture is thin, whip until thickened. The flavour will improve if dip is chilled for at least 24 hours.

Select crisp fresh vegetables for the crudités. Peel and cut into 10 cm (4 in) lengths. Serve chilled with the dip. Suitable crudités are carrots and celery sticks, mange tout (snow peas), radishes, spring onions, blanched broccoli and cauliflower florets.

Serves 6 to 8.

DEVILLED MIXED NUTS

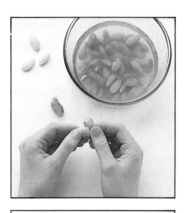

125 g (4 oz) almonds
45 g (1½ oz) butter
2 cloves garlic, crushed
1 teaspoon Worcestershire sauce
2 teaspoons curry powder
pinch of cayenne
125 g (4 oz) raw cashew nuts
125 g (4 oz) pecan nuts
chilli flower. to garnish (optional)

Blanch the almonds by pouring boiling water over the nuts and leaving a few minutes. Lift the nuts out and they will slip out of their skins easily.

Melt the butter and stir in the garlic, Worcestershire sauce, curry powder and cayenne. Sprinkle evenly over all the nuts in an ovenproof dish and toss well to coat evenly with the spicy butter mixture.

Cook at 180C (350F/Gas 4) for 15 to 20 minutes, stirring every 5 minutes to colour evenly. Remove nuts from the oven and cool. Store in airtight container until ready to serve with drinks. Serve in a bowl and garnish with a chilli flower, if desired.

Serves 4 to 6.

SPICED CRACKED OLIVES

1 kg (2 lb) large green olives
2 or 3 red chillies
4 cloves garlic, peeled
3 sprigs each fresh dill, thyme and oregano
2 teaspoons fennel seeds
olive oil, to cover

Make a lengthwise slit in each olive, cutting in as far as the stone. (This allows flavours to penetrate.)

Put olives into a jar with the chillies, garlic, dill, thyme, oregano and fennel seeds. Pour in oil to cover and store, covered in the refrigerator for several days or weeks. Drain and serve as an appetizer with drinks or in salads. More olives can be added to the oil, or the oil may be used afterwards for cooking or in salads.

Makes 1kg (2 lb).

CALAMATTA OLIVES WITH GARLIC
Put calamatta olives (a variety of Greek olive with distinctive flavour), with peeled cloves of garlic in a jar and pour in olive oil or a mixture of olive and vegetable oil. Cover and store in the refrigerator for a few days or several weeks. Drain and serve. The oil may be used for cooking and salad dressings. A few whole chillies may be added to give bite.

ASPARAGUS ROLLS

25 spears fresh or canned asparagus
4 egg yolks
250 g (8 oz) butter
squeeze of lemon juice
1 tablespoon chopped fresh mint
1 loaf unsliced bread

If using fresh asparagus, trim the stalks and cook in a pan of boiling water for 8 minutes. Drain and rinse with cold water. If using canned asparagus drain.

To make the Hollandaise sauce, whip the egg yolks in a food processor until frothy. Melt the butter. When very hot, gradually add to the yolks, in a thin stream, with the processor on all the time. Transfer to a bowl and chill the mixture until thickened. Flavour the Hollandaise with lemon juice to taste and stir in the mint.

Use a serrated or electric knife to cut the bread into 25 thin slices. Cut away the crusts. Spread bread slices with the Hollandaise sauce and place one asparagus spear, cut in half, on each piece. Join two corners of each with a wooden toothpick. Dot with more sauce. Place under a preheated grill and cook until crisp.

Makes 25.

CUCUMBER SANDWICHES

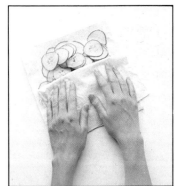

2 cucumbers
3 teaspoons salt
1 loaf sliced white or brown bread
125 g (4 oz) butter
pepper
3 tablespoons thick sour cream
1 bunch snipped fresh chives

Thinly slice the cucumbers. (If using the tough-skinned variety, peel and remove seeds first.) Sprinkle with salt, put a plate and weight on top and leave for several hours.

Drain all the juices from the cucumbers, rinse under cold water to remove excess salt, drain and pat dry between sheets of absorbent paper. Chill until ready to use. Remove the crusts from the bread and butter the slices on one side only. Top half the slices with the cucumber and cover with the remaining slices of bread, buttered side down.

Cut each sandwich diagonally into quarters. Spread the sour cream on one of the cut sides of each triangle and dip into the snipped chives. Arrange on a platter.

Makes 48.

DOLMADES

180 g (6 oz) packet vine leaves
1 onion, finely chopped
2 tablespoons olive oil
500 g (16 oz/2 cups) cooked rice
salt and pepper
2 tablespoons chopped fresh mint
90 g (3 oz/1 cup) toasted pine nuts

Drain the vine leaves, rinse well and soak in cold water to remove the brine, separating the leaves carefully. Drain.

Gently sauté the onion in the oil. When tender, add to the rice and season to taste with salt and pepper. Stir in the mint and half the nuts. Place 2 teaspoons of this filling on each vine leaf, roll up and tuck in the edges.

Pack stuffed vine leaves close together in a shallow pan, making more than 1 layer if necessary, and separating the layers with extra vine leaves. Add enough hot water barely to cover the vine leaves. Place a plate directly on top of the rolls with a can on top to weigh them down. Cover and simmer for 30 minutes. Cool, then chill. Serve garnished with remaining pine nuts.

Makes about 45.

GINGERED FRUIT KEBABS

1 cantaloupe (rock) melon or honeydew melon (or a mixture of both)
125 g (4 oz) strawberries
300 ml (10 fl oz) carton thick sour cream or natural yogurt
1 tablespoon honey
1 tablespoon chopped glacé ginger
1 tablespoon chopped mint

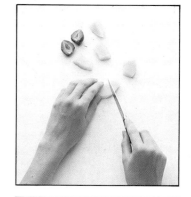

Peel melon; cut in half, scoop out seeds and cut flesh in bite-size pieces. Wash and hull strawberries; halve.

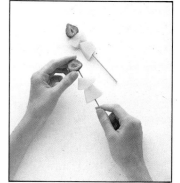

Thread the fruit on to bamboo skewers, alternating the different fruits. If preparing ahead, lay the skewered fruit in a container, cover and chill until ready to serve.

To make the honey sauce, combine the sour cream, honey, ginger and mint. Chill until ready to serve. Turn dipping sauce into a bowl and surround with kebabs.

Makes about 20.

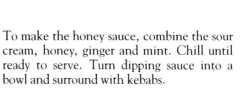

Index